D1409157

GREAT BATTLES THROUGH THE AGES

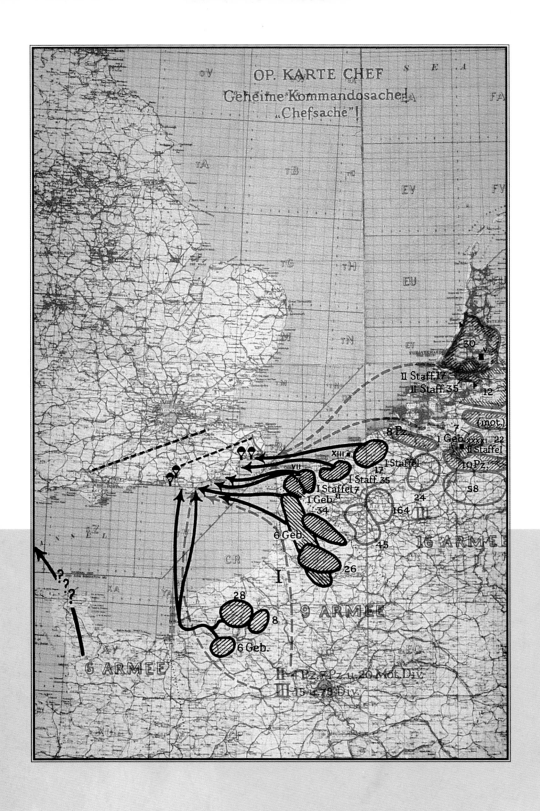

GREAT
BATTLES
THROUGH
THE AGES

SINKING OF
THE *BISMARCK*

SAMUEL WILLARD CROMPTON

**INTRODUCTION BY
CASPAR W. WEINBERGER**

CHELSEA HOUSE
P U B L I S H E R S
A Haights Cross Communications Company
Philadelphia

FRONTIS: In the fall of 1940, German war leaders made plans for Operation Sea Lion, an invasion of Great Britain. As the arrows indicate, the major thrusts were to come directly across the narrowest part of the English Channel.

CHELSEA HOUSE PUBLISHERS

VP, PRODUCT DEVELOPMENT Sally Cheney
DIRECTOR OF PRODUCTION Kim Shinners
CREATIVE MANAGER Takeshi Takahashi
MANUFACTURING MANAGER Diann Grasse

STAFF FOR SINKING OF THE *BISMARCK*

EXECUTIVE EDITOR Lee Marcott
SENIOR EDITOR Tara Koellhoffer
PRODUCTION ASSISTANT Megan Emery
PICTURE RESEARCHER Noelle Nardone
SERIES & COVER DESIGNER Takeshi Takahashi
LAYOUT 21st Century Publishing and Communications, Inc.

A Haights Cross Communications ✦ Company

http://www.chelseahouse.com

First Printing

1 3 5 7 9 8 6 4 2

Library of Congress Cataloging-in-Publication Data

Crompton, Samuel Willard.
    Sinking of the Bismarck / Samuel Willard Crompton.
        p. cm.—(Great battles through the ages)
Summary: Recounts events leading up to and surrounding the May 1941 destruction of the British battle cruiser Hood by the German battleship Bismarck, soon followed by the sinking of the German ship by British forces. Includes bibliographical references and index.
    ISBN 0-7910-7438-2 (hardcover) 0-7910-7793-4 (paperback)
    1. Bismarck (Battleship)—Juvenile literature. 2. Hood (Battle cruiser)—Juvenile literature. 3. World War, 1939-1945—Naval operations, German—Juvenile literature. 4. World War, 1939-1945—Naval operations, British—Juvenile literature. [1. Bismarck (Battleship) 2. Hood (Battle cruiser) 3. World War, 1939-1945—Naval operations. 4. Naval battles.] I. Title. II. Series.
D772.B5C76 2003
940.54'5—dc21
                                                    2003004592

TABLE OF CONTENTS

INTRODUCTION

by Caspar W. Weinberger

There are many ways to study and teach history, which has perhaps been best defined as the "recording and interpretation of past events." Concentration can be on a compilation of major events, or on those events that help prove a theory of the author's. Or the "great man" theory can be applied to write the history of a country or an era, based on a study of the principal leaders or accepted geniuses who are felt to have shaped events that became part of the tapestry of history.

This new Chelsea House series adopts and continues the plan of studying six of the major battles and turning points of wars that did indeed shape much of the history of the periods before, during, and after those wars. By studying the events leading up to major battles and their results, inescapably one learns a great deal about the history of that period.

The first battle, chosen appropriately enough, is the Battle of Actium. There, in 31 B.C., the naval forces of Antony and Cleopatra, and those of Octavian, did battle off the northwest coast of Greece for control of the Roman world. Octavian's victory ended the Roman civil war and gave him unchallenged supremacy, leading to his designation as Augustus, Rome's first emperor. It is highly appropriate that the Battle of Actium be studied first for this series, because the battle was for many decades used as the starting point for a new era.

Next, in chronological order, is a study of the long years of battles between the forces of Richard the Lionhearted and Saladin. This Third Crusade, during the twelfth century, and the various military struggles for Acre and Jerusalem, was the background against which much of the history of modern Britain and Europe and the Middle East was played out.

Coming down to modern times, the series includes a study of the battle that forever changed naval warfare. This battle, the first between two ironclad warships, the *Monitor* and the *Merrimack*, ended the era of naval wars fought by great fleets of sail- or oar-powered ships, with their highly intricate maneuvers. After the *Monitor* and *Merrimack*, all naval battles became floating artillery duels with wholly different tactics and skills required.

The sinking of the German ship *Bismarck* during World War II was not so much a battle as a clear demonstration of the fact that a huge preponderance of naval force on one side could hunt down and destroy one of the most powerful battleships then afloat.

The continued importance of infantry warfare was demonstrated in the Battle of the Bulge, the final attempt of the German army, near the end of World War II, to stave off what in hindsight is now seen as the inevitable victory of the Allies.

The last battle in this series covers the Korean War—one of the most difficult and costly we have fought, and yet a war whose full story is very nearly forgotten by historians and teachers. The story of the Korean War embodies far more than simply the history of a war we fought in the 1950s. It is a history that is dominated by General Douglas MacArthur—but it is also a history of many of the foundation stores of American foreign and domestic policy in the past half century.

These six battles, and the wars of which they were a part, are well worth studying because, although they obviously cannot recount all of history from Actium to Korea, they can and do show the reader the similarities of many of those issues that drive people and governments to war. They also recount the development and changes in technologies by which people have acquired the ability to destroy their fellow creatures ever more effectively and completely.

With the invention and deployment of each new instrument of destruction, from the catapults that were capable of blasting great holes in the walls defending castles and forts, to today's nuclear weapons, the prediction has always been made that the effects and capability of each of those engines of destruction were so awful that their very availability would end war entirely. Thus far, those predictions have always been wrong, although as the full potential of nuclear weapons of mass destruction is increasingly better understood, it may well be that the very nature of these ultimate weapons will, indeed, mean that they will ever be used. However, the sheer numbers of these ultimate weapons possessed by many countries, and the possibilities of some of those countries falling under the dictatorship of some of the world's most dangerous leaders, combine to make imaginable a war that could indeed end the world. That is why the United States has expended so much to try to prevent countries such as Iraq and North Korea from continuing to be led by men as inherently dangerous as Saddam Hussein and Kim Sung Il, who are determined to acquire the world's most dangerous weapons.

An increasing knowledge of some of the great battles of the past that have so influenced history is essential unless we want to fulfill the old adage that those who forget history are likely to be condemned to repeat it—with all of its mistakes.

This old adage reminds us also that history is a study not just of great military victories, but also the story of battles lost and the many mistakes that were made by even the greatest of commanders.

After every engagement that involves American troops in action, even on a very small scale, the Pentagon conducts a "Lessons Learned" exercise. What went wrong? What should have been done differently? Did we need more troops, more artillery, more planes? Most important, could more lives of our own troops have been saved?

These mistakes or command errors are not only carefully studied and written about, but they form the basis for war games or exercises in which actual battle situations are re-fought—sometimes on paper—but frequently with troops re-enacting various parts of the combat action. These "lessons learned" exercises become a valuable part of the training of troops and are an even more valuable part of the training of leaders and commanders.

As we can all guess from the short discussions of some of those great battles in this series, there were many opportunities for different commanders and different plans to be used. Indeed, history is perhaps our greatest teacher, and a study of great battles is a great way to learn, even though each battle is different and there will be different lessons to be learned from the post-battle studies.

So, this Chelsea House series serves as a splendid beginning to our study of military history—a history that we must master if we want to see the expansion and success of our basic policy of maintaining peace with freedom.

It is not enough to consider threats to our security and our freedom. We must also be constantly ready to defend our freedom by keeping our ability to prevent any of those threats against us from materializing into real dangers. The study of great battles and how they were won, despite mistakes that have been made, is a vital part of our ability to keep peace with freedom.

BY: Caspar W. Weinberger
Chairman, FORBES Inc.
March 2003

Caspar W. Weinberger was the fifteenth U.S. secretary of defense,
serving under President Ronald Reagan from 1981 to 1987.

Hitler was at his best addressing political rallies. Here he is surrounded by members of the SS, the most feared and despised of all German combat groups.

Hitler's Gambles

His fifty-second birthday on 20 April was bizarrely celebrated with a concert in front of the Special Train, after Göring had eulogized the Führer's genius as a military commander, and Hitler had shaken the hand of each of his armed forces' chiefs. While there Hitler heard the news of the capitulation of both Yugoslavia and Greece.

—Ian Kershaw, *Hitler: 1936–1945, Nemesis*

Adolf Hitler became the chancellor of Germany in 1933. Born in Austria in 1889, he was not a native German, but he managed to appear "more German" than most natives. He was soon known as the *führer*, which translates as "leader."

Within six years of coming to power, Hitler had become the most powerful and successful German leader since Otto von Bismarck (1815–1898). In the spring of 1941, he was at war, and he wanted to strike another blow at Germany's enemy, Great Britain.

Hitler had always been a gambler—not a reckless one, but an eager one. He had gambled numerous times in his career, and won enough to make others envious. Now, as he celebrated his fifty-second birthday, Hitler was on the verge of taking some more gambles.

First and foremost, he was determined to invade his neighbor to the east, the Soviet Union. Hitler had been allied with Soviet dictator Joseph Stalin for nearly two years, but Hitler despised Russian civilization. He saw the Soviet Union as an immense land of forests, iron, copper, and oil, all of which he believed were needed for the future of Nazi Germany.

Second, Hitler did not to want to allow his Italian ally, Benito Mussolini, to be humiliated. Mussolini had invaded Greece in March, and the Italians had been bogged down in the mountainous terrain, fended off by persistent Greek guerrilla fighters. Hitler intended to sweep over Yugoslavia and Greece, to show the Eastern Europeans just how vengeful he could be.

Third, Hitler believed it was essential to keep the United States out of the war. He had no great admiration for the Americans, but he knew that their intervention had been pivotal in Germany's defeat in World War I, and he wanted to prevent that from happening again. Therefore, he wanted a continued peace, however chilly, with U.S. President Franklin Roosevelt and the Americans.

As he celebrated his fifty-second birthday on April 20, 1941, Hitler was in fact at war with only one major opponent, Great Britain. Up to this point, Hitler had been unable to find a way to penetrate the British defenses.

Between September 1939 and July 1940, Hitler had fought and defeated the Poles, Dutch, Belgians, French, Danes, and Norwegians. Each country had yielded to him after a short, futile resistance. Only Great Britain, safely isolated across the 20-odd-mile (32-odd-kilometer) English Channel had been able to resist Hitler. Even the mighty German *Luftwaffe* (air force) had not found a way to subdue the British.

As he surveyed the situation on April 20, Hitler knew that the initiative still lay in his hands. Although he could not make Great Britain fall, neither could the British force him to give up his massive possessions on the continent of Europe. Hitler wondered whether he should let this stalemate continue.

At this point, Hitler the gambler emerged. A nervousness of mind never allowed Hitler to rest or to consolidate his gains. Whenever he had the choice to wait or to take action, Hitler always chose to make the first move, and he was determined to do so now, to keep the game moving.

So, Hitler would attack Soviet Russia. To do so, however, he first had to follow up where his ally had failed by conquering Yugoslavia and Greece. The German army and air force had already made considerable progress toward this goal, and their accomplishments made the German navy nervous. It did not want to lose out on the chance to obtain some glory in this war.

Two weeks after his birthday, Hitler went to Gotenhafen, the naval port just outside Danzig (what is now Gdansk in northern Poland). He went on board the battleship *Bismarck*, the greatest warship afloat, and probably the most heavily armored warship of all time. It had been built between 1936 and 1939, and it was the pride of the German navy.

Adolf Hitler inspected the *Bismarck* on May 5, 1941. The German führer went aboard and met both Captain

Battleship *Bismarck* was launched in February 1939, but that December, it was still fitting out in port. Because of Hitler's caution regarding naval warfare, *Bismarck* would not see combat until May 1941.

Ernst Lindemann and Admiral Gunther Lutjens. Hitler also made conversation with a number of the common sailors; he had a special affinity for enlisted men, since he had been a lance corporal during World War I. Hitler, Lutjens, and Lindemann had lunch together. The führer was quiet at first, but then he launched into a diatribe against the Soviet Union and the British. He did not say a word about the German navy or its plans. Hitler was, as usual, thoroughly absorbed with land-based military affairs.

Despite being essentially a landsman, Hitler did have some insight into naval matters. To Admiral Lutjens, he expressed concern that British air power might pose the greatest threat to the *Bismarck* at sea. However, Lutjens brushed this argument off, pointing out the *Bismarck*'s great armament.

As he ended his four-hour tour of the great battleship,

Hitler expressed doubts about the future of battleships. He mentioned to one of his aides that U-boats (submarines) could do the same things as battleships, but at a fraction of the cost.

Hitler may have had a point, but this was the *Bismarck*, the greatest battleship in the world. Built between 1936 and 1939, it represented the best of German efficiency and design. The *Bismarck* was nearly 800 feet (244 meters) long, had 15-inch (38-centimeter) guns that could hurl shells up to

Otto von Bismarck

Born in Prussia (a kingdom in Northern Europe that later became part of Germany) in 1815, Bismarck unified Germany. He accomplished what no previous German leader had done since the early Middle Ages; he brought all of the German peoples together under the flag of one nation.

The aristocratic Bismarck became premier, or prime minister, of Prussia in 1862. Like his contemporary Abraham Lincoln, Bismarck believed in national unification; also like Lincoln, Bismarck had to bring his nation together through war. Bismarck greatly increased the size of the Prussian army and equipped it with the new rifles and steel cannons of the 1860s. Then he went to war against Denmark in 1864, Austria in 1866, and finally, France in 1870–1871. All three wars ended with stunning Prussian victories. As a result, Bismarck was able to declare the formation of a new German Empire, with King William I of Prussia becoming the new German emperor. The ceremony was commemorated at Versailles (the city in France that had been home to French royalty), to emphasize the defeat of France and the rise of Germany.

Having accomplished so much through war, Bismarck went on to become a statesman and worked for peace. He kept Germany out of the race to start colonies and an overseas empire, and he worked to ensure good relations with Great Britain. William I died in 1888, however, and his grandson William II fired Bismarck in 1890. During his retirement, Bismarck lamented the aggressive policies of Emperor William II that eventually helped bring on World War I in 1914.

15 miles (24 kilometers), and armor plate that was 15 inches (38 centimeters) thick. It had been named for Otto von Bismarck, known as the "Iron Chancellor" of the Second *Reich* (empire).

Hitler, Lindemann, and Lutjens all knew that the German navy intended to send *Bismarck* out to sea to engage in combat in the near future. What Hitler did not know was the state of desperation among many members of Germany's top naval command. Having endured defeat in World War I, the naval leaders now feared that U-boats would replace battleships; therefore, the German naval leaders were willing to take gambles that Hitler would not have agreed to, had he known about them.

In May 1941, Adolf Hitler was at the peak of his powers. The German *Wehrmacht* (armed forces) had defeated Poland, Denmark, Norway, Belgium, Holland, and France in the past 20 months. The German Luftwaffe had terrified Polish and French civilians, and had nearly done the same to the British. The only significant failure Hitler had endured was that the Luftwaffe had been unable to pound the British Royal Air Force (RAF) into submission. In May 1941, Hitler stood at a position of power that no past European leader—not even Charlemagne or Napoleon—had ever reached. Hitler was about to launch the greatest offensive—and the greatest gamble—of his career. He was about to begin Operation Barbarossa, the invasion of the Soviet Union.

Hitler and Joseph Stalin, the Soviet leader, had signed a nonaggression pact in 1939. Hitler and Stalin had agreed not to fight one another or stand in the way of the other's territorial ambitions. Hitler had made the most of the freedom the pact gave him, conquering most of Western Europe between September 1939 and May 1941. Now, however, Hitler had resolved to break the pact so he could launch Operation Barbarossa, which was intended to overcome the Soviets, capture the capital at Moscow, and reduce the Soviet people to slaves for the great German Third Reich. More than 3 million German fighting men were being sent to the Russian border, and Hitler had set the date of invasion for June 22.

All of these plans made it extremely difficult for the führer to pay attention to naval details. Despite his focus on land tactics, Hitler had always had a fondness for the navy. His interest in submarines showed that he was a naval strategist of some merit. Hitler had gone to Hamburg (a port in northern Germany) in February 1939 to christen the new battleship *Bismarck*, and he had high hopes that his navy would eventually be able to challenge the British for command of the seas. Hitler, however, was too much of a realist to believe that he could do this yet: The German navy's ultimate success would have to come several years in the future. Therefore, in all likelihood, Hitler returned to Berlin (the German capital) to concentrate on Operation Barbarossa, and intended to forget about the navy for a while.

Pragmatism demanded that the German naval officers restrain themselves for the present. The British Royal Navy dominated the Atlantic Ocean, and the British RAF had shown itself to be a powerful fighting force. Germany's top naval officer, Admiral Erich Raeder, wanted desperately to achieve something significant, though. He was about to launch Rhine Exercise, a naval action by the *Bismarck* and the heavy cruiser *Prinz Eugen* (pronounced *oi-gen*).

The early planning that began months before had called for the *Bismarck* and its sister ship, the *Tirpitz*, to move out together. The two had been built at the same docks and were, by a significant margin, the most powerful ships in the world. The *Tirpitz*, however, was not ready to leave, and delay had led to further delay. As he surveyed the situation and considered his budget, Admiral Raeder was convinced that he had to do something now.

Raeder's greatest fear was that the führer would lose patience with the surface navy as a whole. Hitler had recently shown a marked preference for the U-boats, which were cheaper and could be built more quickly. Battleships had always been the pride and joy of the German navy, but that sentiment seemed to be changing. The Wehrmacht had covered itself with glory, the Luftwaffe enjoyed almost unlimited funds, and the U-boats were thriving. Raeder knew that he had to do something on behalf of the navy. He must send out the *Bismarck* and the *Prinz Eugen*.

Just one week after Hitler's visit to the *Bismarck*, the weather changed abruptly. Thick clouds set in over Northern Europe and the North Sea. Raeder decided that the time had come. Under the cover of heavy weather, his ships might make it farther out to sea without being detected. Orders were sent to Gotenhafen.

The man who received the orders was eager and ready. Admiral von Lutjens was a capable, courageous commander, but, according to his subordinates, entirely without humor. Lutjens had recently returned from a very successful cruise in command of the battleships *Gneiseneau* and *Scharnhorst*. Sailing from Germany, Lutjens had sunk more than 110,000 tons of British shipping goods, and had returned safely to the port of Brest in German-occupied France. Now he had command of an even more powerful team: the *Bismarck* and *Prinz Eugen*.

Lutjens and Lindemann piloted their task force out of Gotenhafen on May 19. The two German leaders knew that the odds were stacked against them. The British had about ten battleships scattered throughout European and Mediterranean waters. Still, the German surface fleet was determined to overcome the shame and defeat it had experienced in World War I. It intended to regain its glory and to ensure its place in the annals of the German Third Reich.

This political cartoon appeared in a British newspaper in 1916. It depicts the rivalry between the British and German navies that had gone on during the entire reign of Kaiser William II (1889–1918).

Germany Versus Britain

Bismarck not only created the Reich but also laid the foundation for the Greater Germany of today.

—Adolf Hitler, christening the
Bismarck on February 14, 1939

The rivalry between the German and British navies dated back at least 50 years. The matchup between the two was a classic example of an old professional fighting a newcomer, except that, in this case, the newcomer came with better equipment.

Great Britain had depended on the sea for centuries. Ever since the days of Queen Elizabeth I, who ruled from 1558 until 1603, the British navy had strived to be master of the seas. The British had, in succession, fought the Spanish, Dutch, and French for mastery of the English Channel, the Atlantic Ocean, and the waters of the Caribbean Sea. The British had finally prevailed in the climactic Battle of Trafalgar, fought against the French and Spanish in 1805. From then until about 1900, there was no question that the British navy was the biggest, strongest, and best equipped in the world. The British had the largest navy in the era of sailing, and when sails were replaced by steam around 1860, the British built the best steamships as well. Then came a new rival, imperial Germany.

Because Germany has played such an important role in world events in the last 100 years, people tend to forget that Germany did not become a unified nation until 1871. In that year, Chancellor Otto von Bismarck and King William I declared the new German Empire. Bismarck and William had previously governed the powerful kingdom of Prussia, but after their victories over the Danes in 1864, the Austrians in 1866, and the French in 1871, the two men announced that the German Empire now included both Prussia and its many German-speaking neighbors.

For the next 18 years, Bismarck and William practiced a safe but sure strategy. Though each of them was a staunch nationalist, which meant they believed Germany should be supreme, neither of them wanted to antagonize Great Britain, the great naval and commercial power of the day. When other German leaders declared that Germany needed battleships and colonies of its own, Bismarck said such things were unnecessary. Let the British rule the sea, as Germany ruled the land.

Kaiser (German for "emperor") William died in 1888 and was briefly replaced by his son, Kaiser Frederick III, who continued this policy. Frederick died of throat cancer that same year, however, and was replaced by his son,

Kaiser William II. William II fired Bismarck in 1890 and the old chancellor went into retirement.

William II lacked the patience and stability to direct German affairs wisely. Between 1890 and 1914, he repeatedly created tensions with the British, especially through his buildup of the German navy. By the time World War I began in 1914, the German fleet was about two-thirds the size of the British navy, and represented the first real challenge to Great Britain's naval supremacy in the past 100 years.

German naval officers were bitterly disappointed when William II kept them in port through much of the war. The only major German sally culminated in the Battle of Jutland in 1916. There, the Germans performed very well, inflicting more damage than they suffered. Rather than follow up on the success, however, the kaiser and his advisors brought the fleet back to port, where morale began to sink. It seemed that the kaiser valued his ships too much to risk them in a major engagement.

Parts of the German navy mutinied in 1917. Such rebellions were not unprecedented. Both the German military and the civilian population had suffered intensely during the war. The German navy, however, with its high standards and exalted status, was not where a mutiny would be expected to occur.

There was another, more serious, mutiny in October 1918, just weeks before the end of World War I. Kaiser William abdicated his throne and went into exile in Holland in November, and Germany was left without a leader. In the peace negotiations that followed, the British demanded that the entire German High Seas Fleet sail into Scapa Flow, a sheltered lagoon just above Scotland, and surrender to the British.

The German fleet did sail from its ports. As the fleet sailed into the harbor at Scapa Flow in 1919, though, the

German crews sank their own ships, in full view of the British. The British called this "treachery," but it was an act that followed the tradition of countries with proud navies. A nation did not spend huge amounts of money on battleships only to yield them to an enemy at the end of a war.

The Treaty of Versailles, signed in 1919, did not allow Germany to have a navy in the future. The British wanted no competition from Germany. When Adolf Hitler came to power in January 1933, however, he immediately began a system of national rearmament, which included rebuilding the navy. By the beginning of 1939, the navy that the führer had built was only about one-third the size of Great Britain's, but it was, pound for pound, more heavily armed and equipped. On February 14, 1939, St. Valentine's Day, Hitler christened the battleship *Bismarck*.

The *New York Times* reported the scene the next day. The ship was officially named by Countess Dorothea von Loewenfeld, a granddaughter of Otto von Bismarck. Hitler gave a long speech in which he hailed Bismarck and subtly attempted to claim for himself a position as Bismarck's heir:

> Of all the men who can lay claim to having prepared the way for the new Reich, one stands out in mighty solitude — Bismarck. . . . Bismarck not only created the Reich, but also laid the foundation for the Greater Germany of today.
>
> Despite all restraints he laid the cornerstone for the national Socialist unitarian State.[1]

There must have been some people in the audience who held back expressions of disbelief or snickers of contempt. Bismarck, after all, would never have approved of the state Hitler had created. Bismarck had been a loyal *Junker*

(Prussian nobleman) who believed in the rule of the kaiser, the chancellor, and the Junkers. Bismarck had also opposed the establishment of a large German navy. Bismarck had always believed that it was Germany's destiny to rule Europe, and as long as it did not interfere with his goals, he would let the British continue their dominance of the seas. Once, when someone asked him what he would do if the British landed their army and threatened Germany, Bismarck retorted, "Send a policeman and have it arrested."[2]

The irony was apparent on February 14, 1939. The greatest German battleship was being named in honor of the man who had strongly opposed Germany's "Big Navy" policy. By failing to heed Bismarck's advice, Hitler appeared to be moving toward the same set of mistakes that had been committed by Kaiser William II.

World War II began on September 1, 1939. Hitler's armies invaded Poland, and France and Great Britain declared war on Nazi Germany. Hitler may have made some errors in naval policy, but his opening moves in World War II were nothing short of brilliant. Using a new type of warfare called *blitzkrieg* ("lightning war"), in which troops moved in rapidly without warning, Hitler crushed Poland in 1939, and Norway, Holland, Belgium, and France in the spring of 1940. By the summer of 1940, Hitler held a position higher than anything Kaiser William II had ever enjoyed, even more impressive than what Otto von Bismarck had accomplished. He had only one enemy left, but it was the fiercest and most bitter of Germany's enemies, Great Britain.

Great Britain entered World War II with a small, antiquated army, but with its great navy fully intact. Great Britain had always been able to resist continental dictators in the past, because of its control of the narrow waterways between England and the European continent: the English

Battleship *Bismarck* was launched on St. Valentine's Day of 1939. Hitler and Field Marshal Hermann Göring were present. Europe was then at peace, but Hitler's invasion of Poland that September would start World War II.

Channel. The advent of air power made a great difference, though; if the Luftwaffe could bomb British ships, Hitler might be able to cross the Channel and succeed where others before him had failed.

The Battle of Britain was fought in the air between September 1940 and May 1941. Throughout those months, German planes dropped bombs on southern England. The British RAF scrambled night after night to struggle against the Luftwaffe for control of the air.

For the first month, perhaps even the first six weeks, Hitler and the Germans made steady progress. They successfully attacked British airfields and caught many British planes on the ground. In October, however, Hitler changed tactics. Believing he could pound the British into submission, he redirected the German attacks toward

London and a handful of other British cities. Night after night, the air raid sirens shrilled and Londoners hastened to underground shelters. Many spent their nights in the subway tunnels. Though the Germans caused many casualties and destroyed a number of landmarks, they failed to break the British will to resist. Led by Prime Minister Winston Churchill, the British muddled through the hardship and kept on going. By the late autumn, the British were outfighting the Luftwaffe in the air, and by early spring of 1941, it was apparent that England had won the Battle of Britain. Hitler had suffered his first major defeat.

During the late winter and early spring of 1941, Hitler put the finishing touches on an even more ambitious campaign. Code-named Operation Barbarossa, after Frederick Barbarossa, who had been a German emperor in the twelfth century, the plan called for more than 3 million German troops to sweep into the Soviet Union and reach Moscow by the end of the year. The soldiers would be backed up by the best in German engineering: tanks, planes, jeeps, and cars. This would be the largest military campaign in human history.

Hitler intended for Operation Barbarossa to begin by mid-May 1941, but his timing was upset by some inept performances on the part of Mussolini, his Italian ally. Mussolini invaded Greece in the spring, hoping to show Hitler that he could achieve a swift and stunning success of his own. Instead, the Italians were stuck in northern Greece. Rather than allow his ally to look foolish, Hitler released a large section of German troops to sweep south into the Balkans and complete what Mussolini had begun. The Germans performed with their usual skill, and by mid-May, Greece had been won.

Operation Barbarossa had not been called off, however. It had merely been postponed and given a new start

The Germans pioneered the use of submarines in World War I. Now, in World War II, they used U-boats extremely effectively; millions of tons of Allied shipping were sunk during the war.

date of June 22, 1941. At the same time that he looked forward to his invasion of the Soviet Union, Hitler had to consider both naval forces and the combined land, sea, and air forces.

Greek defenders, who had been joined by units from the British army, fled Greece to the Mediterranean island of Crete, 100 miles (161 kilometers) to the south. Hitler's advisors persuaded him to undertake the first major drop of parachute forces in history, in order to capture Crete. If this could be accomplished, the Germans would be much closer to their eventual goal of taking the oil fields in and around the Suez Canal in Egypt.

The German army had won most of the laurels in the war so far. The submarine unit of the German navy was beginning to outdistance the surface navy in the competition for funding requests. As recently as May 5, 1941, Hitler had confided to an aide that, "The U-boats do these things better and faster, and without such incredible expenditures."[3] Therefore, the leaders of the German navy were desperate to accomplish something in the spring of 1941, to demonstrate their importance to the Reich and to the war effort.

The U-boats

U-boats were intended to operate in packs, rather than alone. Acting in concert, a group of U-boats could converge on a merchant convoy in the North Atlantic and pick off a number of ships while the escort vessels blundered about trying to find the elusive underwater vessels.

The Germans had first deployed U-boats in World War I. A U-boat had located and sunk the merchant ship *Lusitania* in 1915; that one act nearly brought the United States into the war. The Germans and British had argued bitterly over what was proper conduct in U-boat warfare. According to the British, a U-boat should surface, announce its presence, and search merchant ships for contraband (forbidden goods). If it was found, then the Germans had the right to sink the ship. To the German U-boat captains, such a policy seemed clearly to be suicidal. They believed it was imperative for them to hit and sink their targets without warning.

Right from the start of World War II, the U-boat packs won Hitler's confidence and admiration. He lavished more praise and money on the U-boats than on the surface fleet, and in so doing, he caused the leaders of the surface navy to fear for their budgets and their ships. One consequence was that Admiral Raeder sent the *Bismarck* and *Prinz Eugen* out prematurely; another was that Admiral Lutjens did not feel safe returning to Germany after winning his first battle against H.M.S. *Hood*. The pressure exerted by the U-boats harmed the British war effort; that same pressure also forced the German naval command into compromising situations.

Breakout to the
Denmark Strait

Battleship *Bismarck* is seen in the background. This photograph was taken from the decks of heavy cruiser *Prinz Eugen* in May 1941, just before the Rhine Exercise commenced.

I give you the hunter's toast: Good hunting and a good bag!

—Captain Lindemann to the *Bismarck* crew

The German air force began an aerial bombardment and a parachute invasion of Crete on May 20. Air Marshal Hermann Göring committed the best (some might say the most fanatical) of the German parachute troops to the invasion. The British defenders had had numerous warnings that an attack was coming, but nothing could have prepared them for the fury with which the Germans made their assault. As British Prime Minister Winston Churchill later wrote:

The Germans used the whole strength they could command. This was to be Göring's prodigious air achievement. It might have been launched upon England in 1940 if British air-power had been broken. . . . When the battle joined we did not know what were the total resources of Germany in parachute troops. The 11th Air Corps might have been only one of half a dozen such units. It was not until many months afterwards that we were sure it was the only one. It was in fact the spear-point of the German lance.[4]

Churchill made the Germans sound weaker than they actually were. He wrote these words years later, and with a sense of relief. As he pointed out, no one knew how many parachute divisions the Germans had, or whether they intended to use Crete as a place from which to leapfrog through the eastern Mediterranean on their way to Egypt and the Suez Canal.

On the same day that the invasion of Crete began, two German warships sailed from Gotenhafen, the port just outside of Danzig. These were the *Bismarck* and the heavy cruiser *Prinz Eugen*. At noon on May 20, Captain Ernst Lindemann addressed the *Bismarck* crew by loudspeaker:

The day that we have longed for so eagerly has at last arrived: the moment when we can lead our proud ship against the enemy. Our objective is commerce raiding in the Atlantic, imperiling England's existence. Let us hope for great success. I know that it has been, and will continue to be, the crew's sincerest desire to participate directly in Germany's final victory. I give you the hunter's toast: Good hunting and a good bag![5]

Lindemann's confidence in his crew was justified. The more than 2,300 sailors and marines aboard the *Bismarck* were eager for a contest with the British enemy. Lindemann,

Winston Churchill (right) was the British prime minister during
World War II. Born in 1876, at the height of the Victorian Age when
Great Britain was one of the world's greatest powers, he was
determined not to let the British succumb to the threat posed by
Nazi Germany.

however, had not told his men about all the perils and
obstacles they would confront as they edged into the North
Sea. Lindemann was also not in complete charge of the
operation. He was the captain and leader of the *Bismarck*, but
on the deck above him was Admiral Gunther Lutjens. Not

only did Lutjens outrank Lindemann, but Lutjens was the commander of the entire Rhine Exercise, which included the *Bismarck* and the *Prinz Eugen*. Lutjens, although known to be efficient and brave, was also morose and laconic; he would seldom confide his thoughts to the captain of the *Bismarck*.

Surprise was vital to the success of the *Bismarck* and *Prinz Eugen*. That evening, though, just eight hours after Lindemann addressed his crew, the British admiralty in London received an encrypted (coded) message from its contacts in Stockholm, Sweden: "Most Immediate. Kattegat today 20th May. At 1500 [hours] two large warships escorted by three destroyers, five escort craft, ten out of twelve aircraft passed Mastrand course northwest 2058/20th May/1941."[6]

Hardly 100 miles (161 kilometers) from home port, the two German ships had been sighted and reported. The British admiralty did not make an immediate response. The British already had their hands full, and they also wanted confirmation before sending ships in a new direction. Still, the alert had been passed.

The *Bismarck* and *Prinz Eugen* steamed north with a cover screen of seven merchant ships around them. There were numerous German airplanes flying over, to demonstrate that the Luftwaffe would support the ships in the Rhine Exercise. Despite how smoothly the operation seemed to be going, there was already some consternation on the part of Captain Lindemann and Captain Helmut Brinkmann of the *Prinz Eugen*. Both captains found it nearly impossible to win the ear or the confidence of Admiral Lutjens.

A veteran of World War I, Lutjens was aloof by nature. He tended to answer requests with a simple "yes" or "no," usually giving the latter answer. Lutjens almost never provided reasons for his responses. In that way, he was a throwback to the German navy of World War I. German leaders were expected to make swift decisions and not to justify them to their subordinates.

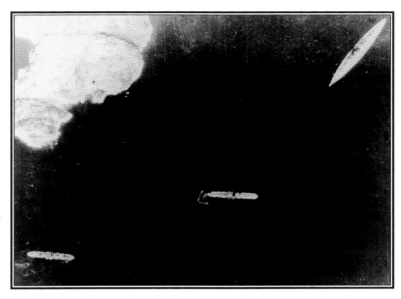

A British spy plane took this snapshot of *Bismarck*, on the right, and *Prinz Eugen*, on the left, as the two ships began their wartime exercise. British air power played an important role throughout the *Bismarck* campaign.

Both Lindemann and Brinkmann were also veterans of World War I. They had adjusted with the times, however; each of them was known as convivial by his crew, a hearty and happy spirit. By contrast, the fleet commander was dour and unapproachable.

Bismarck, *Prinz Eugen*, and their merchant convoy gingerly picked their way through a minefield left by the British. Having cleared the field, the ships made their way rapidly up the Norwegian coast and anchored in the harbors around Bergen, Norway, on May 20.

Everything appeared to have gone well to this point, but Lutjens and Lindemann soon received some disconcerting messages from Berlin. The British were clearly aware of any movement by the German fleet, and may even have been alerted to this particular operation. Late that afternoon, a British spy plane circled over Bergen Harbor and confirmed that the *Bismarck* and *Prinz Eugen* were not only out of port, but were about to break into the North Sea.

British intelligence converged at the admiralty head-quarters in downtown London, and the messages were then routed north to the Home Fleet headquarters at Scapa Flow. Located ten miles (16 kilometers) off the northern Scottish coast, Scapa Flow was—and still is—a gloomy place for sailors. Far removed from the pleasures of home ports, Scapa Flow was nonetheless the perfect spot for the naval headquarters: Ships could leave Scapa Flow and con-verge on the coast of France, the Lowlands, or Norway in a matter of hours. Scapa Flow had been the center of British operations during World War I, and it was here that the Germans had scuttled their fleet in 1919, rather than hand it over to the British.

Commander of the Home Fleet Sir John Tovey was 56 years old in 1941. He had gone to sea at an early age and gained glory at the Battle of Jutland in 1916. Tovey's audacious maneuver there had saved the British fleet additional losses. At the beginning of World War II, Tovey had served in the Mediterranean. Again, employing bold tactics, he had charged and routed a superior Italian fleet, and by the autumn of 1940, he had become commander-in-chief of the Home Fleet.

This was an awesome responsibility. Tovey had to watch the Germans at all times, he had to respond to U-boat attacks, he had to guard merchant convoys, and he had to provide escorts for troop convoys (a very large one was now bound for Egypt). This was not the type of job at which Tovey excelled; he was at his best leading his men into heroic action, rather than reacting to the moves of the enemy. In fact, Tovey had already made one important mistake this year.

Just four months earlier, in January, Tovey had learned that Admiral Lutjens had ventured out with the *Scharnhorst* and *Gneiseneau*. These were important German battleships, though not part of the top class occupied by the *Bismarck*. Tovey had accurately anticipated that Lutjens would head for the Denmark Strait between Iceland and Greenland. Tovey had waited for Lutjens just south of the strait, with a naval force that far surpassed the *Scharnhorst* and *Gneiseneau*. Lutjens had identified the British ships just in time to avoid sailing into the trap; he had returned north, and the British had had to go back to port for more fuel. In that interval,

Bismarck's Specifications

It was the largest, heaviest, and most powerful warship in the world. It had been designed by the best German marine architects, and yet, like all ships throughout history, it had its weaknesses.

The *Bismarck* was 823 feet (251 meters) long, 118 feet (36 meters) wide, and displaced slightly more than 50,000 tons. It had a triple-turbine power plant that could reach 150,170 horsepower, and it had a maximum speed of slightly more than 30 knots. *Bismarck* could hold 8,294 tons of fuel and 160 tons of lubricating oil. It held enough food to feed a city of 250,000 people for an entire day.

Bismarck carried eight 15-inch (38-centimeter) guns. It could hurl its 1,764-pound (800-kilogram) shells more than 38,000 yards (34,717 meters). Its secondary artillery consisted of twelve 6-inch (15-centimeter) guns, intended for use against enemy destroyers. The ship was protected by 17,569 tons of armor plate, making it by far the densest ship in the world. Even so, there were weaknesses.

Bismarck had traditional steam-turbine engines, rather than diesel engines. Its armor plate was magnificent, but not designed with "plunging fire" in mind. (Plunging fire is delivered from a higher elevation toward a lower target.) *Bismarck* had radar equipment, but it could only detect the existence of other ships: it could not determine their location or range. Perhaps most important of all was its Achilles's heel: *Bismarck*'s twin rudders. No British architect noted the flaw, and no British plane aimed for the rudders, but they were there, all the same—a major flaw in the otherwise mighty *Bismarck*.

Lutjens had sailed into the Atlantic and attacked merchant ships. He sank a total of 22 ships before he brought the *Scharnhorst* and *Gneiseneau* into port at Brest, France, in March. This successful cruise had enhanced Lutjens's reputation — and harmed Tovey's. The only consolation, from the British point of view, was that the *Scharnhorst* and *Gneiseneau* were now under close observation at Brest by the British air force.

Tovey was now at Scapa Flow and Lutjens was at Bergen, Norway. On May 22, Lutjens ordered his task force to sail from Bergen. The *Bismarck* and *Prinz Eugen* left behind the merchant ships that had been their cover and headed due west, toward the four straits that led into the North Atlantic. Luckily for the Germans, a low-pressure weather system had set it in, providing excellent cloud cover for their ships. In his typical fashion, Lutjens did not inform either Lindemann or Brinkmann of his intentions.

German High Admiral Erich Raeder spent that day in the Bavarian Alps with Adolf Hitler. Raeder spoke to the führer for some time about recent successes achieved by the German U-boats, and only slipped in, at an opportune moment, the news that *Bismarck* and *Prinz Eugen* had made their way out of the Baltic Sea and were about to commence raiding British commercial ships.

Hitler was angry, to say the least. He had visited *Bismarck* just three weeks before, and Raeder, Lutjens, and Lindemann had said nothing about this upcoming campaign. Hitler lectured Raeder about the danger posed by British air power and reminded Raeder that the presence of German ships in the North Atlantic might provoke the United States to assume a more warlike posture against Nazi Germany. Displaying the keen intuition that had brought him so many victories in recent years, such as the invasions of Poland, Norway, and France, Hitler suddenly demanded, "*Herr Grossadmiral*, if at all possible, I would like to recall the ships."[7]

Grand Admiral Erich Raeder (left) is seen here making an inspection of a German naval vessel. Raeder was frustrated by Hitler's faith in the power of U-boats and his reluctance to utilize traditional major battleships.

Despite Hitler's request, Raeder stood his ground. He told the führer that the plans for Rhine Exercise had been under way for a long time and that the *Bismarck*'s preparations had been extensive. To recall the ships at this point would be deadly for the morale of the navy.

Hitler reluctantly gave his consent to the plan. He confided to Raeder, however, that he had a very bad feeling about the whole business. Then he let the matter drop. He had to. He was in the process of launching an air invasion of the island of Crete, and was also putting the finishing touches on what would be the largest land invasion in human history: Operation Barbarossa against the Soviet Union.

As he left, Raeder may have congratulated himself on having presented his führer with an accomplished fact, one that Hitler could not alter. Raeder had taken a great risk, though, both in regard to his relationship with the führer and concerning the lives of the thousands of sailors aboard the *Prinz Eugen* and *Bismarck*.

The Mighty
H.M.S. *Hood*

4

H.M.S. *Hood* was the pride of the British navy. Launched in 1918, it was the strongest ship afloat during the years between the two world wars. A young British signalman, Ted Briggs, was elated to have the chance to serve aboard the *Hood*.

Give us the news and we will finish the job.

— Winston Churchill, in a telegram to Franklin Roosevelt

L aunched in 1918, H.M.S. *Hood* was the pride of the British navy. It displaced 48,000 tons, was 860 feet (262 meters) long, and carried eight 15-inch (38-centimeter) guns. All this made it the world's most powerful ship until the launching of the *Bismarck*, and both the British and their foes looked on the *Hood* with a degree of awe. Most of the German sailors aboard *Bismarck* and *Prinz Eugen* had, in the course of their training, carried out mock battles against imaginary British opponents, and most of the time the *Hood* was the enemy ship. *Hood* was named for Admiral Samuel Hood, who had fought the

41

French in both the Caribbean and Mediterranean from the mid-1700s until his death in 1814. Hood had been the foremost of all British naval commanders until he retired and was superseded by Horatio Nelson, who had been one of his protégés.

One of the sailors aboard *Hood* was Ted Briggs, a young signalman. Many years later, Briggs recalled what impelled him to join the navy, and what led him to his post aboard *Hood*. He had been only 13 years old when *Hood* had visited the area where he lived:

> It was in the mid-1930s. She came up the mouth of the Tees. Local fishermen were charging five shillings a time to row people round her and I badly wanted to go. My mother, being a widow, couldn't afford the money and I remember crying my eyes out that I couldn't afford it. The majesty of her [the *Hood*] registered—I decided then and there that I wanted to join the navy. I went round to the recruiting office and they patted me gently on the head and said, "Come back when you're fifteen." Seven days after I was fifteen I joined HMS *Ganges*, the training ship.[8]

By a series of fortunate accidents, Briggs had been posted to H.M.S. *Hood*. As a signalman, he had the honor of hoisting the flag to officially begin the war with Germany in September 1939. Now, though still young, he was a seasoned sailor, and he was on board *Hood* as it traveled to where the admiralty believed the *Bismarck* and *Prinz Eugen* were located.

Briggs and his 1,500 fellow sailors knew that theirs was one of the world's most famous ships, but they were unaware of some of its faults. The *Hood* had weaknesses that were unknown to the Germans, and which the British had gone to some lengths to conceal. First, the ship's deck armor was too thin to hold against shots that might be fired by enemy battleships. Its long, sleek appearance concealed the fact that it was vulnerable to hits in the bow. All the same, *Hood* was the

This signed photograph of Admiral Sir John Tovey was given to his niece, Third Officer Nancy Tovey, during World War II. She often acted as the admiral's chauffeur when he visited the naval base at Scapa Flow.

centerpiece of any British naval strategy, and it was now the center of plans to catch the *Bismarck*.

Admiral John Tovey had a great many ships under his command, but most of them were dispersed when the word came that *Bismarck* had broken out of the North Sea. Tovey set to sea himself aboard the battleship *King George V*, but his main hope lay with H.M.S. *Hood* and H.M.S. *Prince of Wales*, both of which were patrolling the Denmark Strait.

Tovey could not cover all entrances to the North Atlantic, but he stationed himself at what he perceived to be the most vulnerable: the Faroe Islands, north of Scotland.

A large convoy of troops was scheduled to leave Clyde, Scotland, on May 22. Tovey made sure that the troops were well escorted, but he knew the possibility remained that the *Bismarck* might somehow slip around British defenses and attack those ships full of enlisted men. Tovey had been chastened by the German success in February, when *Scharnhorst* and *Gneiseneau* had evaded him. He could not afford another such humiliation, and the British Empire, strained to the brink, could not afford to let the *Bismarck* run loose in the Atlantic, sinking convoys. Therefore, Tovey ordered an enormous convergence of British naval forces to prevent any breakout.

At or near Scapa Flow, Tovey had two battleships, one battle cruiser, two 8-inch (20-centimeter) gun cruisers, eight 6-inch (15-centimeter) gun cruisers, and 12 destroyers. This firepower seems immense when compared to just two German ships, but Tovey had to be prepared to cover thousands of miles of ocean, while the Germans only needed a space of 20 to 30 miles (32 to 48 kilometers) to evade the British. There was yet another factor that figured into Tovey's calculations: fuel.

Tovey and most of the men who served under him had grown up in a time when the British navy controlled over half the coaling stations in the world. Because of these holdings, the navy had not quickly adapted to the new opportunities offered by oil, and the tanks of most British ships were much smaller and lighter than those of the Germans. To be sure, it was still an advantage to control so many coaling and refueling spots, but the British were to some extent handicapped by their own success. The Germans, knowing that the British controlled the seas, had long since adapted to heavier oil tanks, and as a result, the *Bismarck* could outrun and outlast almost any British ship afloat.

All this tended to keep Tovey at anchor in Scapa Flow. If he sailed immediately, he and his squadron might run out of fuel just when they needed it most. So Tovey waited until the evening of May 22, when aerial reconnaissance confirmed that the *Bismarck* and *Prinz Eugen* were no longer in Norwegian waters.

Tovey then set out at once. He divided his fleet so that all four approaches to the North Atlantic would be covered. The news quickly reached Prime Minister Winston Churchill, who took the opportunity to telegraph U.S. President Franklin Roosevelt:

> Yesterday, 21st, *Bismarck*, *Prinz Eugen*, and eight merchant ships located in Bergen. Low clouds prevented air attack. Tonight they have sailed. We have reason to believe that a formidable Atlantic raid is intended. Should we fail to catch them going out, your Navy should surely be able to mark them down for us. *King George V*, *Prince of Wales*, *Hood*, *Repulse*, and aircraft-carrier *Victorious*, with ancillary vessels, will be on their track. Give us the news and we will finish the job.[9]

Churchill's message was encouraging something that Adolf Hitler feared intensely. Hitler had explicitly told his top naval officers not to provoke the Americans. Churchill, for his part, was counting on the bond between the Americans and the English to bring the United States into the war. Franklin Roosevelt admired the British and detested Nazi Germany, but the isolationist movement in the United States, which opposed entering the war, was strong enough to prevent Roosevelt from joining the English to fight Germany.

Ironically, just one day before Churchill sent his telegram, a U.S. ship had been fired upon by Germans for the first time in the war. The merchant ship *Robin Moor* had been cornered by the German submarine U-69 off the

Members of the crew of H.M.S. *Hood* line up for company inspection. Morale was high aboard the *Hood*, but the ship had never been fully tested in battle and the bow area's vulnerability to plunging fire caused some concern.

coast of Brazil. The U-boat commander followed the rules of engagement that had been laid down in World War I. He surfaced and demanded the ship's papers. After these revealed that there was war materiel on board, the U-boat captain gave the ship's crew 30 minutes to scramble into lifeboats. Then, he sank the *Robin Moor*. Because the incident took place in a remote area and it took some time for the crew to be rescued, Roosevelt and the U.S. government did not learn of the event until June 10.

Meanwhile, on the *Bismarck*, Lutjens continued to speak

little to either of his ship captains. As the *Bismarck* and *Prinz Eugen* continued due west, they ran into heavy fog, which provided good cover against British spotter planes. The *Bismarck*'s meteorologist suggested to Lutjens that they increase ship speed to take full advantage of the cloud cover. Lutjens brusquely refused. The meteorologist expressed his frustration to gunnery officer Mullenheim-Rechberg: "He won't budge. He simply rejects the idea without giving any reasons."[10] That was Lutjens's trademark style.

Throughout May 22 and most of May 23, the German ships made rapid progress across the North Sea and Denmark Sea. The low-pressure weather system that had set in about a week earlier continued to cover them from British planes and ships.

On the evening of May 23, German lookouts shouted that they had seen enemy craft to starboard (the right side of the ship). The German ships were carefully picking their way through the Denmark Strait when they were seen and identified by the British heavy cruiser H.M.S. *Suffolk*. The *Suffolk* was followed by H.M.S. *Norfolk*, both of which swiftly cabled the *Bismarck*'s position to London. If the Germans had still had the advantage of any element of surprise, it was now gone.

At 8:30 P.M., Captain Lindemann had his gunner open fire on the *Norfolk*. The shots straddled the *Norfolk*, which quickly withdrew to a safer position. The first shots of the *Bismarck*'s cruise had been fired.

All night long, Admiral Lutjens and Captains Lindemann and Brinkmann maneuvered, trying to throw off the British pursuit. None of their moves succeeded; the British hung on to *Bismarck*'s tail all night, sending countless messages to the admiralty in London about the German position. Meanwhile, Admiral John Tovey and the rest of the British Home Fleet were making every effort to catch up with the elusive enemy.

This painting shows one of the most dramatic moments of the entire war in the Atlantic region: the sinking of H.M.S. *Hood*. Only three men survived the destruction; among them was Ted Briggs.

Battles of Iceland and Crete

Hood's *blown up, sir.*

—British admiralty report, conjectured by C.S. Forester
in *The Last Nine Days of the Bismarck*

The German task force made its way through the Denmark Strait on the night of May 23–24, 1941. Dawn comes early in those latitudes, and at about 5:30 A.M., German voices barked out an alarm: "Enemy ships, enemy ships!"

To the southeast, about 20 miles (32 kilometers) away, two British ships were headed on a collision course with the *Bismarck* and *Prinz Eugen*. For about ten minutes, Admiral Lutjens's staff argued about the nature of these ships. Were they battle cruisers?

Destroyers? Finally, the staff arrived at the dreaded conclusion: These were battleships.

All night long, Vice Admiral Lancelot Holland had been closing in on the Germans. Alerted first by Admiral Tovey and then by the admiralty that the *Norfolk* and *Suffolk* had located the German ships, Vice Admiral Holland had altered his direction and was now closing in fast on H.M.S. *Hood* and H.M.S. *Prince of Wales*.

The element of surprise had now tipped to the British side. Admiral Lutjens showed no sign that he was stunned by the sight of the British battleships, but inwardly, he knew

Radar

In 1904, Christian Huelsmeyer received a patent for the first device to locate ships and trains in fog using radar. As often happened, however, German technology wavered under the pressure of World War II and the loss of numerous scientists, particularly Jewish ones, to democratic nations.

In 1936, the British set up a series of radar locations along the coast, to guard against possible air attacks. The system was expanded in 1940, the year British scientists definitively gained an edge over their German counterparts. By late 1940, many British warplanes were equipped with radar devices, and by early 1941, radar had become an important part of the defense system of the Home Fleet, headed by John Tovey.

By contrast, the Germans lagged during 1940 and 1941. There was competition for radar contracts, and the Luftwaffe demanded priority for its radar system. The German navy went without to a large extent. *Bismarck* sailed with optical range finders, but without the type of radar that would have enabled it to find and sink British ships in bad weather.

Admiral Lutjens conceded the importance of radar in one of many messages to the naval high command. The British use of radar, he stated, was making probes and sorties into the Atlantic much more difficult than before. The German navy might have time to get back its advantage, but it was too late for *Bismarck*, which was not only outnumbered on the high seas, but had to sail blind in comparison to its British foes.

at once that the information he had received from Berlin had been faulty, and that the British had better naval intelligence. To make matters worse, Admiral Raeder had issued Lutjens a set of conflicting orders on Lutjens's departure. Lutjens was to concentrate on shipping convoys, and to proceed with caution and deliberation. However, if he should be engaged by large enemy forces, he must fight to the finish.

Lutjens spent the next 15 minutes wavering between these two orders. As the British plunged toward the Germans with heavy seas surging up over the bows of their ships, Lutjens kept on a course that would lead past the British to the open Atlantic. Lutjens would have liked to avoid action here, but Vice Admiral Holland forced it upon him.

As they charged straight toward the Germans, the British could only fire their fore-guns. Even so, since they had two battleships against the Germans' one battleship and one heavy cruiser, the British had a slight advantage in their number of heavy guns. They began to fire at 6:00 A.M.

For several minutes, Lutjens continued to falter as if he were overcome by paralysis. As British fire kicked up the seas around his ship, Lutjens held his course and refused all requests by his chief gunnery officer to fire. Then, as if he had been concealing this intention all along, Lutjens pulled a brilliant maneuver by altering course to port. Suddenly, both the *Prinz Eugen* and *Bismarck* were in an excellent position to fire. The British changed course, too, but in the two or three minutes it took them to make the maneuver, they presented themselves to the enemy. Now, Lutjens gave the order to fire.

Bismarck's heavy guns roared and belched in the morning air. The thunder from the guns could be heard as far away as Reykjavik, Iceland. *Bismarck*'s first salvo fell short, its second scored a small hit or two, and on the fifth, its gunners found their mark. H.M.S. *Hood* staggered under the blow.

This photograph, taken from the deck of H.M.S. *Prince of Wales*, is the last known photograph of H.M.S. *Hood* as it steamed off to meet the *Bismarck*.

At this moment, because of his maneuver, Lutjens had his two ships firing across each other's line of fire. *Bismarck* was firing on *Hood*, and *Prinz Eugen* was firing on the *Prince of Wales*. It looked as if it would be a long morning, when suddenly, H.M.S. *Hood* began to disintegrate before the eyes of the British sailors and the German enemy. One of the best accounts of what followed was given by a gunnery officer aboard the *Bismarck*.

> The sight I saw then is something I shall never forget. At first the *Hood* was nowhere to be seen; in her place was a colossal pillar of black smoke reaching into the sky. Gradually, at the foot of the pillar, I made out the bow of the battle cruiser projecting upwards at an angle, a sure sign that she had broken in two.[11]

H.M.S. *Hood* sank minutes later. Only three men out of its crew of 1,500 were saved. One of them was signalman Ted Briggs. He was unable to inflate his lifejacket, because it was under his waterproof coat. Briggs later recalled the moment:

> B turret was just going under . . . that was about 50 yards [46 meters] away. I panicked and I turned and swam as fast as I could away from her. There were lots of 3-foot [one-meter] square Carly rafts. . . . I managed to get on one of those. I turned and looked and by that time she'd [the *Hood*] gone, but there was a fire on the water where she'd been. Now the water was about 4 inches [10 centimeter] thick with oil, and again I panicked and turned and swam as fast as I could, paddled the raft as fast as I could away from here, and when I looked round again the fire had gone out. [12]

Two other men who had survived joined Briggs. The three men held out for hours aboard their rafts, until they were rescued by the destroyer *Electra*.

Both the Germans and the British were in awe at the sight. The Germans were triumphant and amazed; the British were dismayed and in shock. H.M.S. *Hood* was gone.

Years later, famous naval historian C.S. Forester gave a fictional account of how the news was received at the British admiralty in London.

The last words were called forth by a sight of the messages already spoken down the voice-pipe now delivered by pneumatic tube. The rear admiral hardly glanced at it.

"Most immediate report from *Suffolk*," announced the officer at the voice-pipe: "*Hood* and *Bismarck* opening fire. *Hood*'s course approximately southwest.

"*Hood*'s closing in on her," said the rear admiral. Once more he paid almost no attention to the written signal handed him.

"Most immediate signal from *Suffolk* coming through," said the young officer. He was clearly pretending not to be excited; he was making a show of iron calm. And in that moment all his calm disappeared. He seemed to wilt. "What's that? Repeat that." He sat at the voice-pipe doing nothing for a moment.

"Get on with your job, man," snapped the rear admiral.

The young officer turned a face of tragedy towards him.

"*Hood*'s blown up."

"What?"

At this moment the written message rattled down the tube. A dozen hands reached for it and the rear admiral tore it from the container.

"*Hood* blown up," he said. "*Hood* blown up."[13]

With the hindsight of more that half a century, the loss of H.M.S. *Hood* does not seem as tragic today as it did to the British high command on May 24, 1941. Today, it is known that Adolf Hitler had already committed his forces to more than half a dozen battlefronts and that just four weeks later, he would make the supreme error of invading the Soviet Union. To the men at the British admiralty on the morning of May 24, however, the world looked dark indeed.

Meanwhile, Hitler's invasion of Crete was rapidly picking up speed. On May 25, the decision would be made to evacuate the surviving British defenders there. On top of that defeat, the Germans had blown up the *Hood*, which had been the symbol of British naval might for the past 23 years. It was a grim moment for the British high command.

At the same time, there was jubilation aboard the *Bismarck*. Lutjens and Lindemann congratulated each other, while German sailors shouted and yelled excitedly. This was probably the single greatest ship-to-ship victory that the German navy had yet won over its British opponent.

Even in the midst of the great victory, there was a division of opinion among the German commanders. Captain Lindemann first asked then practically begged Admiral Lutjens to commence a chase of H.M.S. *Prince of Wales*, the remaining British warship. Lindemann was confident that he could catch up to the *Prince of Wales* and destroy it within three to four hours.

In his position as commander-in-chief of the task force, Admiral Lutjens looked at matters from a strategic viewpoint. Lutjens, too, was excited by the victory, but he remembered the orders from Admiral Raeder, that hunting British convoys was his primary objective. Lutjens refused Lindemann's impassioned appeal, and both men then learned that the *Bismarck* had taken some hits during the artillery duel.

The *Bismarck* had taken a shot to one of its fuel compartments, and the ship was already leaving a visible trail of oil. Considering how important it was for the great ship to have ample fuel reserves and how far it was from home base, this was a significant problem. Once again, C.S. Forester

Members of *Bismarck*'s crew participate in a refueling drill. Although *Bismarck* had huge oil tanks, the ship's remarkable speed caused oil to burn rapidly. This contributed to Admiral Lutjens's decision to head toward Brest, France, rather than continue the Atlantic cruise.

provides a semifictional account of a conversation between Lutjens and Lindemann:

> "There's still plenty of time to go back, sir," suggested Lindemann.
>
> "I understand that, too," said the admiral. "Thank you, Commander."
>
> Lutjens and Lindemann stood staring at the map.
>
> "Two hundred tons less oil," said Lindemann— "and that's a permanent loss sir, while we stay at sea. When we meet our tankers, it will be two hundred less that we shall be able to take on board."
>
> "Yes," said Lutjens, still thinking deeply. His forehead was sweeping out arcs on the chart. He talked more to himself than to Lindemann. "The decision I have to take—the next words I say—can change the

history of the world, can decide the fate of nations, can settle the destiny of Germany and of National Socialism and of our Führer. Ten thousand—twenty thousand—fifty thousand lives can be cut short by my next order."

"That is so, sir."

"Forward—back. This is the last moment in which to choose. No changing of minds after this."

"I've given you my opinion, sir."

"No!" said Lutjens suddenly. "I shall go forward. We haven't fought our way out into the Atlantic just to go back again tamely. Forward! We shall have to turn aside into Brest [a port in northwestern France]. Two days there and the damage can be repaired. Then, with the *Scharnhorst* and the *Gneiseneau*, I shall sail out again at the head of a squadron incomparable for power and speed."[14]

Lutjens had decided. The *Bismarck* would continue on its quest. There remained, however, that troubling loss of oil. Lutjens ordered Lindemann to get away from the British cruisers—*Norfolk* and *Suffolk*—to the rear. Lutjens then reported to Berlin that he had sustained some damage in the battle and that he needed to head for the western coast of France for repairs.

By now, the news of *Hood*'s destruction had reached Berlin as well as London. Admiral Raeder, exultant over the news, telephoned Adolf Hitler to deliver the tidings. Hitler received the news rather impassively; he was less elated than Raeder might have expected. Hitler still had a sense of foreboding about the entire enterprise, but still, he did not order that the ships return to Germany. The führer was preoccupied with the invasion of Crete.

The Crete invasion had been launched on May 20, just as *Bismarck* was poking its way into the North Sea. Hitler wanted a swift, decisive victory, but the British controlled

At almost exactly the same time that *Bismarck* fought *Hood*, German paratroopers landed on the Mediterranean island of Crete. The Germans achieved remarkable success there, but at the price of many of their best paratroop units.

most of the waterways between Crete and the mainland of Greece. Luftwaffe leader Hermann Göring convinced Hitler that this was the time to make use of the German paratroopers; they had not played an important role in the defeat of either France or the Low Countries (the Netherlands, Belgium, Luxembourg, and the northwest of France). Now was their chance to shine. Hitler concurred, and starting on the morning of May 20, Göring had hurled the very best of his 7th division paratroopers against the British on Crete.

The fighting was fierce from the outset. The British and New Zealand units on Crete had been instructed to do their utmost to prevent a German takeover. Crete appeared to be a logical territory for the Germans to conquer on their way to Cyprus and then on to the Middle East. If their luck held, the Germans might then approach the Suez Canal from two directions. Erwin Rommel's *Afrika Korps* would attack from Libya, while the German air force would continue its drive south.

May 23 was a bad day for the British defenders on Crete. Though they inflicted heavy losses on the German paratroopers, the British lost two cruisers and had three destroyers sunk, and one battleship damaged and put out of action for the moment. On May 24, the very day that the *Bismarck* engaged and sank *Hood*, the British chiefs of staff sent the following telegram to their leader on Crete:

> Our difficulties in Crete are great, but from all the information we have, so are those of the enemy. If we stick it out the enemy's effort may peter out. . . . The vital importance of this battle is well known to you, and great risks must be accepted to ensure our success.[15]

The German paratroopers were coming closer on Crete. The situation looked grim from the British side.

Admiral Gunther Lutjens celebrated his fifty-second birthday during *Bismarck*'s cruise. Despite his victory over H.M.S. *Hood*, Lutjens remained fundamentally gloomy and pessimistic.

Turn for France

"Hard a-starboard!," was quickly followed by "Hard a-port!"
as Bismarck *zig-zagged in rapid motion.*

Admiral Lutjens knew almost nothing about what had happened at Crete. The German high command did not readily share information between its different parts. Therefore, the German navy was not alerted to the invasion of Crete, which was a display of the German air force. In retrospect, all this secrecy and interservice rivalry appears to have hindered the German effort.

Lutjens did know that the *Bismarck* needed repairs, and he was about to make a large turn in direction, to head toward the coast of France. If he could make his turn undetected, and if he had just one or two days of good (in this case, cloudy) weather, he should be able to reach the cover of the German air force, which was operating out of France. Again, this entailed a type of inter-service cooperation that was rare in the German military.

Considering the odds against him, Admiral Lutjens had done remarkably well up to this point. He had crossed the North Sea, passed the Denmark Strait, and reached the Atlantic Ocean. He had just won one of the most notable successes ever achieved by a German warship. Even so, Lutjens knew how perilously close his margin for error had been. He also knew that the führer was exceptionally unforgiving toward commanders who did less than what he considered their duty. It may be that Lutjens plunged ahead into the Atlantic rather than risk Hitler's wrath on his return. In any event, Lutjens sent a laconic message to Captain Brinkmann on the *Prinz Eugen*:

> Intend to shake off contact as follows: *Bismarck* will turn away on a westerly course during rain squalls. *Prinz Eugen* to maintain course and speed unless forced to turn away or 3 hours after *Bismarck* has turned. Thereafter, release to refuel from *Belchen* or *Lothringen*. Then conduct independent cruiser warfare. Execute on signal "Hood."[16]

Again, there is little fault to find with Lutjens's strategy. He had shown his brilliance in maneuvering the *Bismarck* during the battle with *Hood*. He now chose a clever strategy that, if successful, might shake off the British cruisers. The criticism that can be leveled is that Lutjens did not consult with either Lindemann or Brinkmann before he made this decision.

Lutjens had counted on almost everything except British aircraft. This was a blind spot for Lindemann. Back on May 5, when the führer had visited the *Bismarck*, Hitler had expressed concerns about British air superiority, and Lutjens had brushed them off. War has a way of making and shaping technology, though, and planes that took off from aircraft to attack ships were about to become a permanent feature of World War II.

H.M.S. *Prince of Wales* participated in the pursuit of *Bismarck*. The British temporarily lost contact with *Bismarck* but reestablished it after an overflight by a torpedo plane.

The *Bismarck* and *Prinz Eugen* parted company. The *Prinz Eugen* set a course due south and was soon in the clear, but the *Bismarck* continued to be dogged by two ships: the cruiser *Norfolk* and H.M.S. *Prince of Wales*. Even worse for the Germans, H.M.S. *Victorious* was now close enough to launch its Swordfish planes against the enemy.

The Swordfish were hardly state-of-the-art planes; they were relics from the latter stages of World War I. On the evening of May 24, however, H.M.S. *Victorious* launched nine Swordfish. They flew over H.M.S. *Norfolk*, confirmed *Bismarck*'s position, and then attacked *Bismarck* as it steamed along south by southeast.

Consternation prevailed aboard *Bismarck*. The crew, which had been on alert and at battle stations for 36 hours, now had to respond to swift and desperate commands from Captain Lindemann. An order of "Hard a-starboard!" was quickly followed by "Hard a-port!" as *Bismarck* zigzagged in rapid motion, trying to escape the torpedoes carried by the Swordfish planes. At the same time, all of *Bismarck*'s antiaircraft guns were firing at once. Even the 15-inch (38-centimeter) guns were used to fire into the sea, kicking up enormous fields of spray to deflect the planes.

All but one of the Swordfish planes returned safely to the decks of H.M.S. *Victorious*, but the pilots brought little good news. There had been perhaps one hit on *Bismarck*'s port side, but no obvious damage. The British had only the mixed consolation that, for the first time in naval warfare, planes had successfully taken off from an aircraft carrier and attacked a capital ship (one of the largest types of fighting ships) on the open sea.

Admiral Lutjens was deeply shaken by the Swordfish

Aircraft Carriers

The battleship was the preeminent form of naval warship between 1870 and 1940, but the first two years of World War II showed the importance of the new "flat top," or aircraft carrier. The British had converted *Ark Royal*, a merchant ship, into their first aircraft carrier in 1914, and the U.S.S. *Langley*, a collier (ship for transporting coal), was converted and launched in 1922. The world's first true aircraft carrier, however, was H.M.S. *Hermes*, launched in 1923. Many naval leaders were skeptical of the new type of warship, despite the convincing demonstration of air power made at Hampton Roads, Virginia, in 1921, when planes attacked and sank a German battleship that had been delivered to the Allied powers.

At the beginning of World War II, Great Britain and the United States had most of the world's aircraft carriers, with Japan coming in a distant third. The German government had, with good reason, concentrated upon U-boats and a handful of battleships such as the *Bismarck*.

Three events helped the aircraft carrier come into its own. First were the aerial attacks made upon the *Bismarck*, which slowed its progress toward France. Second was the Japanese attack on Pearl Harbor, Hawaii, six months later. Third was the Japanese sinking of two British battleships in the China Sea solely through air power. By the start of 1942, most naval planners around the world conceded that the aircraft carrier had replaced the battleship as the single most vital instrument of naval warfare. One of the last hurrahs for the traditional battleship came in April 1945, when the Japanese ship *Yamato* approached U.S. naval forces. *Yamato* came under intense fire from the air and eventually sank with almost its entire crew. One of the few survivors, Yoshida Mitsuru, later wrote *Requiem for Battleship Yamato*, published in 1985.

attack. Just 16 hours earlier, he had been exultant in his victory over H.M.S. *Hood*. Now he was thoroughly on the defensive, trying to dodge two British navy ships, and he had been attacked from the air. Through the hours of the night, the German admiral was profoundly ill at ease, and his lack of sleep may have begun to catch up with him.

Bismarck's crew celebrated its good fortune in having destroyed the *Hood*. One gunnery officer remembered that once the "all clear" was sounded at 8:30 P.M., he and other officers gathered to congratulate first gunnery officer Adalbert Schneider. The men drank glasses of champagne and the gunnery officers were in high spirits. That was not the case, however, for their admiral on the bridge.

At around 2:00 A.M., Lutjens came close to panic over the continued presence of the British "shadowing" ships. Rather than collapse under the strain, he instructed Captain Lindemann to carry out a daring maneuver; the Germans would suddenly turn west and then north, and end up behind their pursuers. Then, if all went well, they would set a course due east for St. Nazaire, France.

The plan worked to perfection. At 3:06 A.M. on May 25, the British still had radar contact with *Bismarck*, and occasionally even visual contact. By 3:30 A.M., they had lost all contact with the German battleship, and could only marvel at how it had eluded them.

The German movement was brilliantly executed; it confirms Lutjens's reputation as a daring tactician. As night gave way to morning, though, Lutjens failed to appreciate how fortunate he had been. He continued to believe that the British were following him with radar. In that belief, he forgot to be careful about use of the wireless radio, and sent a number of messages to the German command post in Paris. The radio transmission men there did their best to persuade the admiral that he was in the clear and to stay off the radio, but inexplicably, Lutjens continued to send one message after another.

Lost in the
Great Ocean

Knowing that *Bismarck* was close to safety in France, H.M.S. *Ark Royal* launched Swordfish planes to locate and disable *Bismarck*. The first attempt failed.

The attack must have been almost over when it came,
an explosion aft. My heart sank.

— Gunnery officer aboard the *Bismarck*

Admiral Lutjens could not believe his own luck, that he had escaped the British net. For their part, the British admiralty planners were beside themselves as hours passed without any sighting of the German battleship.

From 3:06 A.M. onward, the British had no real sense of where *Bismarck* was. Admiral John Tovey, aboard the *King George V*, was probably only about 100 miles (161 kilometers) southwest of *Bismarck*, but he did not know that, and he was forced to keep radio silence so as not to give away his position. Lacking any central command on the water, all of the British ships took their cue from the admiralty headquarters in London, which knew even less about the situation.

The weather, too, had turned against the British. The same low-pressure system that had guarded *Bismarck* on its way through the Denmark Strait now made visibility poor throughout the North Atlantic, which compounded the British problems. By about noon on May 25, many of the British naval leaders were in a state of some despair over *Bismarck*. They simply had no idea whether it had turned east or west.

Unwittingly, Admiral Lutjens came to their rescue. Still believing he was being tracked, Lutjens sent a half-hour-long message to German naval headquarters in Paris. Every British detector in the North Atlantic tuned in, and within about half an hour, the British had determined *Bismarck*'s position to within a range of 50 miles (81 kilometers). The information was rapidly forwarded to Admiral John Tovey, who took it to his naval planners. Looking at the data, they concluded that Lutjens was making for the Faroe Islands, the swiftest way back to Germany. Tovey immediately changed course and headed northeast, in full pursuit.

He was going the wrong way. Whether it was a failure on the part of those who had detected the *Bismarck*'s message, or whether the error was made by Admiral Tovey's analysts, the *Bismarck* was plunging through heavy seas to the southeast, while Tovey and the main pursuit were headed northeast.

This was *Bismarck*'s best opportunity to make a full escape. It had just one obstacle left in its way: Task Group A, which was steaming northwest from Gibraltar. Vice Admiral James Sommerville, leading the force, was ordered to station himself just off the Spanish coast and to watch the Bay of Biscay. He had with him H.M.S.

Ark Royal, which had about 60 planes aboard, though not all were operational.

It was then that Lutjens made his second mistake of the day. At noon on May 25, which happened to be his fifty-second birthday, Lutjens went on the loudspeaker to address the crew. Lutjens hailed the crew for its work against H.M.S. *Hood*, but warned that the enemy would follow them all the way to France. Lutjens concluded with the ominous words, "For us seamen, there is now but one cry: Victory or Death."[17]

It was precisely the wrong message to give to the crew. The men of the *Bismarck* were exhausted. They had stayed at battle stations for about 48 hours. They needed something to cheer about, something to hope for. Lutjens gave them not a shred of comfort.

Once again, the fleet chief was at odds with his captain. Lindemann went on the speaker later that afternoon and attempted to cheer his crew. He said that they would soon trick the British and dock at a French port. Although they did not cheer wildly, the crew was at least somewhat encouraged by Lindemann's words.

At 4:30 P.M., an announcement from the admiral's bridge—not delivered by Lutjens himself—gave real cause for hope. It was declared that by noon of the next day—May 26—the ship would be within the zone of control operated by U-boats, and that the Luftwaffe would fly out from France to provide air cover. At last, the crew had reason to believe it might survive and be rewarded for its heroic efforts. That hope was not to be fulfilled. The Luftwaffe was still expending most of its strength in the Battle of Crete. Even worse, plunging waves and low visibility soon ruled out any action off the coast of France for May 26. Admiral Lutjens and the crew would have to make it through another day on their own.

One has to wonder about Hitler's state of mind at this

point and question whether or not he realized what was at stake. Did he not see the vital importance of bringing home the *Bismarck*, which had won such a notable victory just one day before? Hitler was neutral, at best, toward his navy. He always placed more trust in the U-boats and the air force than the navy. Second, the interservice rivalry that permeated the German high command did not allow for the type of single-minded, all-out effort that might have saved the *Bismarck*. One simply cannot imagine the British high command doing so little to save the pride of its fleet in similar circumstances.

The British needed a stroke of luck, and it came their way on May 26. At around 10:30 A.M., a U.S.-built Catalina HBY, flying from H.M.S. *Ark Royal*, spotted the *Bismarck*, which was unaccompanied and plunging rapidly southeast toward St. Nazaire, France. The *Bismarck* let fly a barrage of antiaircraft fire, but the Catalina escaped, and soon the news was out: The *Bismarck* was moving southeast as fast as it could; it was not moving northeast.

It seemed a little late to undo the damage, but Admiral Tovey immediately turned the *King George V* around and headed south. He had been led on a wild-goose chase, but he was a determined fighter who never gave up hope. What hope the British now had depended upon the men and planes aboard H.M.S. *Ark Royal*. It was extremely unlikely that they could sink *Bismarck* from the air, but if they could damage it, force it to slow down, there was an outside chance that the rest of the fleet could then catch and destroy it.

At 4:00 P.M., 15 Swordfish planes were launched from the *Ark Royal*. The sea was rough and the *Ark Royal*'s bow was moving as much as 50 feet (15 meters) up and down with each wave. Still, the planes took off, and headed for the *Bismarck*, which was believed to be about 50 miles (81 kilometers) away.

As the planes neared their target, their commander aboard *Ark Royal* suddenly blurted out in English — not in code — "Watch out for *Sheffield*!"[18] It was too late.

Admiral Sir James Sommerville headed the Mediterranean squadron that steamed north from Gibraltar to meet *Bismarck*. His major concern was whether there would be enough time to catch the German battleship before it reached Brest, France.

The pilots of the Swordfish were already attacking H.M.S. *Sheffield*, a light cruiser that had been shadowing *Bismarck* for the last two hours. The planes descended from the clouds and dropped their torpedoes straight at *Sheffield*.

Captain Charles Larcom of the *Sheffield* understood both what had happened and his own peril. He navigated the *Sheffield*, just as a hostile commander would have done, hard to starboard and hard to port, and managed to avoid the torpedoes. One or two came close, but ultimately, the incident proved harmless. The Swordfish then saw, too late, what they had done and flew away, back to the decks of *Ark Royal*.

There was no time for anger or recriminations. As soon as the Swordfish reached *Ark Royal*'s deck, they were brought out and prepared for a second desperate action. Everyone from Vice Admiral James Sommerville to the lowest deckhand knew that this was the last chance. Under cover of night, *Bismarck* would get closer to the French

This photograph of the rudder of a Cunard superliner demonstrates one of *Bismarck*'s weaknesses—in fact, the one that caused the ship's downfall. When its rudder was damaged in the Swordfish attack, *Bismarck* could no longer maneuver in the open sea. It became a sitting duck for the British pursuers.

coast. At some point on the next day, there would be scads of Luftwaffe planes ready to escort it in to St. Nazaire.

The British planes took off at 7:30 P.M. on May 26. There were 15 Swordfish, this time equipped with their regular torpedo hangers. Again, the Swordfish had to cover 50 miles (81 kilometers), but this time there was no mix-up with *Sheffield* or any other ship. The British descended on *Bismarck* at about 8:20 P.M., with just a few streaks of daylight left in the sky.

Voices rang out all over *Bismarck*: "Alarm! Planes to port!" The commanders were at the ready, turning the vessel from starboard to port as necessary, but the men had reached the limit of their endurance. Three days spent at battle stations and three days on mixed rations had taken their toll. Though *Bismarck* put out a noisy antiaircraft fire, the shooting was neither coordinated nor effective.

All the Swordfish returned to the decks of *Ark Royal*. They reported two, perhaps even three hits, but the pilots were not certain about what they had accomplished. The pilots did not know, but aboard *Bismarck*, Lieutenant Burkard von Mullenheim-Rechberg knew. He described the moments following the air attack:

> The attack must have been almost over when it came, an explosion aft. My heart sank. I glanced at the rudder indicator. It showed "left 12 degrees." Did that just happen to be the correct reading at that moment? No. It did not change. It stayed at "left 12 degrees." Our increasing list to starboard soon told us that we were in a continuous turn. The aircraft attack ended as abruptly as it had begun.[19]

Bismarck had two enormous twin rudders. They had been hit by one of the torpedoes, and *Bismarck* rapidly lost its ability to turn. Try as they might, repairmen could not free the rudder, and as the last of the daylight faded, *Bismarck* began to drift helplessly north by northeast, toward the enemy rather than away.

The Nazi flag with its swastika design flies proudly from the aircraft carrier *Graf Zeppelin*. The swastika became one of the most hated symbols of the German Third Reich.

In for the Kill

We all snapped our hands to our caps,
glanced at the flag, and jumped.

—A survivor of the *Bismarck*

During the night of May 26–27, British destroyers hounded the *Bismarck*. They made no major hits against the great battleship, but kept it on its destructive course, headed straight into the arms of the entire British battle fleet. The effort expended in fighting off the destroyers exhausted the *Bismarck* crew; the men had reached the limits of human endurance.

By midnight, Admiral John Tovey learned that the *Bismarck* could no longer maneuver in the heavy seas; it was trapped, headed straight toward him. The British may not have known that the exact cause was the rudder, but they knew that the *Bismarck* was disabled and coming their way. Tovey planned an enormous "welcome" for *Bismarck* on the morning of May 27.

Aboard the *Bismarck*, pessimism had turned to despair, which had yielded to fatalism. Admiral Lutjens, a veteran of many sea fights, knew that this one would be his last. Captain Lindemann, perhaps furious at his chief's refusal to accept his advice about the course of the cruise, was also ready to give up. The 2,200 rank-and-file seamen aboard the *Bismarck*, however, were decidedly not ready to surrender. They were a young crew, averaging about 20 or 21 years of age. Many of them had only recently graduated from Hitler Youth programs, and they were full of the promise of the Third Reich, as it had been described to them by Nazi propaganda.

At 8:00 A.M., gunnery officer von Mullenheim-Rechberg went to the captain's bridge, where he found

Baron von Mullenheim-Rechberg

Born in Spandau, Germany, in 1910, Mullenheim-Rechberg came from a family with a long tradition of military and naval service. He joined the German navy in 1929, and was assigned to the *Bismarck* in 1940 as a gunnery officer.

Aboard *Bismarck*, Mullenheim-Rechberg also served as adjutant to Captain Lindemann, for whom he had great admiration. Mullenheim-Rechberg fired guns during the battle with *Hood*, participated in the attempt to reach France, and, with a handful of other sailors, jumped over the side of the ship shortly before *Bismarck* went down.

That was not the sum of his life, however. Mullenheim-Rechberg was held as a prisoner of war in Canada. He returned to Germany after the war was over, and started a second career as a German diplomat.

Lindemann in a state of complete passivity. This was not the captain von Mullenheim-Rechberg knew, but, as he later put it, "he had been on the bridge of his helpless ship for eleven hours straight. The rudder hit, the destroyer attacks, it was all too much."[20] Mullenheim-Rechberg also passed Admiral Lutjens, who, as usual, did not reveal how he felt about the situation. Half an hour later, the *Bismarck*'s alarm bells began to ring. The battle had started.

Admiral John Tovey had assembled almost the entire Home Fleet for this last attack. *Ark Royal* and Sir James Sommerville's squadron stood respectfully off to the south; they knew that Tovey and his men wanted to get their revenge for the *Hood*. The only problems Tovey and his men faced were time and oil: Virtually all of their ships were near the end of their fuel supplies. The Germans, however, knew nothing of that; they only knew that a large fleet of ships surrounded them. Then the shooting began.

H.M.S. *King George V* led the firing, but it was soon followed by *Prince of Wales*, *Dorsetshire*, and several other ships. For a time, perhaps 15 minutes, *Bismarck* replied furiously. Its 15-inch (38-centimeter) guns belched smoke and flame. Because *Bismarck* could not really turn, however, much less maneuver, it was a sitting duck, and the British guns soon found their marks. Gun turrets aboard *Bismarck* were disabled, passageways crashed into the sea, and compartments leaked badly. Still, the mighty ship refused to sink.

Admiral Tovey broke off the action at 10:15 A.M. He had no choice; his tanks were running out of fuel. Turning north by northwest, he barely made it to home port before running out. Tovey regretted having to leave while the *Bismarck* was still afloat, but he ordered a handful of destroyers to finish the job.

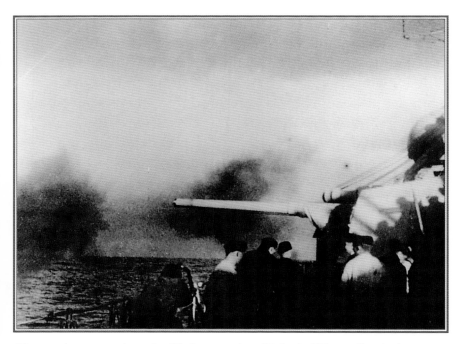

Bismarck was equipped with impressive 15-inch (38-centimeter) guns, but it came under fire from numerous British ships. Unable to turn and run, *Bismarck* and its crew simply endured the terrible pounding that morning of May 27, 1941.

Hundreds of miles away, Prime Minister Winston Churchill reported to the House of Commons at 11:00 A.M. The House met at an alternate location, since its usual chamber had been badly damaged in a German air raid on May 10. Churchill was receiving rapid transmissions of news from the battle, but he had heard the news of *Bismarck*'s demise. Therefore, he told the House:

> This morning shortly after daylight the *Bismarck*, virtually at a standstill, far from help, was attacked by the British pursuing battleships. I do not know what were the results of the bombardment. It appears, however, that the *Bismarck* was not sunk by gunfire, and she will now be dispatched by torpedo. It is thought that this is

now proceeding, and it is also thought that there cannot be any lengthy delay in disposing of this vessel. Great as is our loss in the *Hood*, the *Bismarck* must be regarded as the most powerful, as she is the newest, battleship in the world. [21]

Churchill sat down, then rose immediately and asked the permission of the House to speak again. He said, "I have just received news that the *Bismarck* is sunk." [22]

It had happened at 10:40 A.M. The great ship had gone to the bottom of the sea. The House of Commons roared its approval. So, too, within hours, did the rest of the British nation.

The story of the last minutes of the *Bismarck* can best be told by one of the few survivors, Baron von Mullenheim-Rechberg:

> We all snapped our hands to our caps, glanced at the flag, and jumped.
>
> In the water we were pushed together in a bunch, as we bobbed up and down like corks. At first we swam away from the sinking ship as hard as we could to escape her suction. When I got clear by some 150 meters [164 yards], I stopped and turned around for one last look and to take in everything I could about her.
>
> What I saw was that the *Bismarck* was listing still more. She had no stability left. She was also deeper down by her stern, her bow rearing steeply out of the water. The whole starboard side of her hull, all the way to the keel, was out of the water. I scrutinized it for signs of battle damage, and was surprised that I saw no trace of any. Her port side had borne the brunt of the battle, and that side of her hull may have told a different story.

When swimmers close to the bow of the ship looked back, they saw Lindemann standing on the forecastle in front of turret Anton. His messenger, a seaman, was with him. Soon, both men went forward and began climbing a steadily increasing slope. Lindemann's gestures showed that he was urging his companion to go overboard and save himself. The man refused and stayed with his commanding officer until they reached the jack staff. Then Lindemann walked out on the starboard side of the stem which, though rising ever higher, was becoming more level as the ship lay over. There he stopped and raised his hand to his white cap.

The *Bismarck* now lay completely on her side. Then, slowly, slowly, she and the saluting Lindemann went down. Later a machinist wrote, "I always thought such things happened only in books, but I saw it with my own eyes." The time was 1039 and the battleship's position was approximately 48 10' north and 16 12' west. [23]

By this point, all was chaos. The British, who moments before had been firing at the Germans, now scrambled in close to pick up survivors. There were many, perhaps 800, men in the Atlantic waters. Mullenheim-Rechberg was one of the lucky ones; he was pulled out early and soon found himself on board H.M.S. *Dorsetshire*. Heroic stories are told of these last moments. In one, a British sailor jumped overboard to save a German sailor whom he saw clutching a rope with his teeth; the German had lost both arms in the combat. Many more such tales of heroism might have been recounted had the British commanders not received an urgent warning of nearby U-boats. Following naval policy, the British steamed away from the location, leaving more than 700 men to perish in the water; only 115 had been saved before the U-boat warning came.

One of the last photographs of *Bismarck*. The crew of 2,200 men had fought valiantly but in vain. *Bismarck* broke up and sank at 10:40 A.M.

As it turned out, there was only one U-boat in the vicinity. Its crew managed to rescue only three other survivors from *Bismarck*. The vast majority, well over 90 percent of the 2,300 men who had sailed from Gotenhafen on May 19, died that day, either from gunfire, explosions, or drowning.

The magnitude of the disaster registered very quickly with the German high command. The officers knew that *Bismarck* was incomparably more important to the small German navy than *Hood* had been to the British. Still, they did their best to put a good face on the situation. Orders went out to all the German newspapers: "Reports about

Seen here are some of the survivors from the German crew. They were interred in prison camps in England and Canada. Some of them are still alive today and are part of a veterans' association in Germany.

the *Bismarck* may not exceed two columns. Commentary must be manly, without much pathos."[24]

Hitler's reactions were mixed. One Nazi diarist felt that Hitler seemed little troubled by the loss of the *Bismarck*, while another believed that the führer and the entire high command were deeply downcast over the loss. The German people were another matter. They had just grown used to the idea that *Bismarck* had sunk the *Hood* when the news came that *Bismarck* itself had been destroyed. Given the name *Bismarck* and its historic symbolism to the German Reich, the loss was probably greater than can be imagined today. Even so, Nazi propaganda managed to smother most of the concern with news of recent victories in Crete.

Franklin D. Roosevelt was already famous for his radio addresses before World War II began. On May 27, 1941, he delivered a stern warning to the Nazis by radio and declared a state of unlimited national emergency within the United States.

Hitler Versus Roosevelt

Unless the advance of Hitlerism is forcibly checked now, the Western Hemisphere will be within range of the Nazi weapons of destruction.

—Franklin Roosevelt in a radio address, May 27, 1941

*B*ismarck sank at 10:40 A.M. on May 27, 1941. That very day, Franklin Roosevelt put the finishing touches on a speech that he had spent weeks preparing. Roosevelt had once before postponed the speech; now he seized the moment to make a stand with Great Britain against Germany.

One of the few things that Roosevelt, Winston Churchill, and Adolf Hitler shared was a great speaking ability. Roosevelt's "fireside chats" were renowned in the United States; Churchill's radio addresses were already the stuff of legend; and Hitler had long ago proven himself to be a master of the spoken word, whether on the radio or in front of the *Reichstag* (German parliament). Tonight, it was Roosevelt's turn, and he made the most of it. Roosevelt said,

> My fellow Americans of all the Americas, my friends. . . . The first and fundamental fact is that what started as a European war has developed, as the Nazis always intended it should develop, into a war for world domination. Adolf Hitler never considered the domination of Europe as an end in itself. European conquest was but a step toward ultimate goals in all the other continents. It is unmistakably apparent to all of us that, unless the advance of Hitlerism is forcibly checked now, the Western Hemisphere will be within range of the Nazi weapons of destruction. [25]

Roosevelt went on to portray Hitler and the Nazis as an insane gang of criminals. The president emphasized the importance of the freedom of the seas, and stressed that so long as Germany did not have mastery of the seas, its desires for world domination would remain unfulfilled. Roosevelt had been assistant secretary of the navy during World War I, and he used this naval experience to make his point clear:

> But if the Axis powers fail to gain control of the seas, then they are certainly defeated. Their dreams of world domination will then go by the board; and the criminal leaders who started this war will suffer inevitable disaster. Both they and their people know this—and they and their people are afraid. That is why they are risking everything they have, conducting

desperate attempts to break through to the command of the ocean. Once they are limited to a continuing land war, their cruel forces of occupation will be unable to keep their heel on the necks of the millions of innocent, oppressed peoples on the Continent of Europe; and in the end, their whole structure will break into little pieces. [26]

Roosevelt went on to declare an unlimited state of emergency, which allowed him great powers as president and commander-in-chief. He called upon labor unions and management teams to work together to resolve disputes in view of the crisis, and he asked all Americans to "place the nation's needs first in mind and in action to the end that we may mobilize and have ready for instant defensive use all of the physical powers, all of the moral strength and all of the material resources of this nation." [27]

Roosevelt had spoken. This was his strongest attack against Hitler to date, and no one could mistake the thrust of his message. The *New York Times* headlines of May 28 focused on three items: Roosevelt's speech, the sinking of the *Bismarck*, and the continued struggle for the island of Crete. Americans were now more fully aware of the war and its risks than they had been just one or two months before. The isolationist movement had not lost all of its strength, but most newspaper editorials hailed Roosevelt's speech.

Hitler did not respond to Roosevelt's verbal assault. The führer was occupied with Crete and with trying to fathom what had gone wrong aboard the *Bismarck*. As usual, Hitler did not look to himself or even to the garbled German chain of command to find out what had gone wrong. When Admiral Raeder reported to Hitler on June 6, the führer asked why the *Bismarck* had not turned around immediately after it sank the *Hood* and why it had not pursued and destroyed the *Prince of Wales*. These two questions were at odds with one another, but the führer often expected his subordinates to do the impossible. Hitler did not seem dismayed over the loss of 2,300 German seamen; he was only upset that the navy had acted without consulting him and that one

America First

Many Americans believed they had won World War I for the Allied cause. Whether or not this was true, and it is debatable, many people believed the United States needed to stay out of World War II, and not to repeat the mistake of intervention. Some of the most vehement of the isolationists belonged to groups and committees collectively known as the America First movement.

President Franklin Roosevelt knew the power behind the America First movement. As late as October 1940, he assured reporters that American boys would not be sent to fight in any foreign war. This promise was untruthful. Roosevelt had always believed that Hitler and the Nazis must be defeated; he was simply waiting for public opinion to shift so that he could enter the war.

The spring and summer of 1941 saw the America First movement reach a climax. While Roosevelt and Hitler sparred over submarines and convoys in the North Atlantic, the America First movement held rallies and protests in all major American cities. One of the most prominent leaders of the movement was Charles A. Lindbergh, who in 1927 became the first man to fly solo across the Atlantic Ocean.

In October 1941, Lindbergh gave a disastrous speech in Chicago. He made slighting references to Jews, he questioned the integrity of the Roosevelt administration, and he made himself look ridiculous. Roosevelt seized the advantage. He denounced Lindbergh to the press, damaging the man's reputation, and along with it, the America First movement.

When the United States entered the war in December 1941, Lindbergh volunteered for duty. He helped Henry Ford design planes during the war, but he never overcame the damage to his name associated with his October 1941 speech.

of the capital ships had been lost. Hitler told Raeder that there would be no future sorties into the Atlantic, and that naval policy might soon come under more direct scrutiny. The matter ended there.

The Battle of Crete ended on June 1, 1941. The British carried off the last of their troops in an evacuation that left the island to the German invaders. On paper, it was another impressive Nazi victory, but historians generally portray the invasion as a Pyrrhic victory (one that costs more than it is worth). The German Luftwaffe expended its very best paratroopers in the effort to take the island, and both the Luftwaffe and the German navy was exhausted from the task. If Hitler had followed up the taking of Crete with an invasion of Cyprus or Syria, he might have eventually reached the oil fields and the

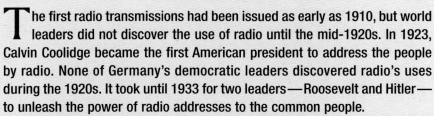

The Power of Radio

The first radio transmissions had been issued as early as 1910, but world leaders did not discover the use of radio until the mid-1920s. In 1923, Calvin Coolidge became the first American president to address the people by radio. None of Germany's democratic leaders discovered radio's uses during the 1920s. It took until 1933 for two leaders—Roosevelt and Hitler—to unleash the power of radio addresses to the common people.

Roosevelt was an aristocrat, but on the radio, he seemed to be the friend of the average person. Hitler, on the other hand, was obsessed with ideas of racial supremacy, but his more unattractive characteristics were masked by radio.

Hitler's speechmaking became less inspired as the years went by. Just one day after the *Bismarck* was sunk, and one day after Roosevelt's radio broadcast, the British Broadcasting Corporation (BBC) made the following comment: "We will let you hear the voices of Roosevelt and Hitler, the voices of the judge and the criminal. . . . We leave it to you listeners to judge which voice is the voice of calm strength and which that of hysterical violence."

Suez Canal. Instead, Hitler was focused on his invasion of the Soviet Union.

As usual, Hitler was about to raise the stakes in the war. Even though Erwin Rommel and the Afrika Korps were about to make good progress, and even though Air Marshal Göring was about to consolidate his success with the capture of Crete, Hitler's thoughts had turned eastward. Everything now depended on his new gamble: Operation Barbarossa against the Soviet Union.

On June 22, 1941, just 26 days after *Bismarck* was sunk, Hitler launched the largest invasion in human history. Three million German troops crossed the Soviet border. Hundreds of German planes strafed Russian villages and thousands of German tanks moved in menacing columns to the east. This was the greatest of Hitler's many gambles; he believed he could overwhelm the Soviets in a lightning campaign, and thereby create a set of German colonies to the east.

Winston Churchill was delighted by the turn of events. For weeks, indeed for months, he had been warning Soviet leader Joseph Stalin that a German invasion was coming. Stalin had ignored the warnings, trusting in Hitler's good will and in the Soviet military. Now Churchill had been proven right.

The Soviets staggered under the invasion. Three million Russians were killed or captured in the first month. Even so, the Soviets fought on. Unlike the Poles in 1939 and the French in 1940, the Soviets had vast lands in which to retreat, as well as great reserves of manpower on which to rely. The Soviets yielded town after town and continued to suffer horrific casualties, but they continued to fight.

The Soviets were not only aided by geography, but also by the British. Immediately after Operation Barbarossa began, Churchill addressed the House of Commons and told the House that he believed Great Britain had to aid the

HITLER'S SIX MONTHS IN RUSSIA

SINCE June 22, Hitler has lost about 2,000,000 troops, killed and wounded, but has taken only 400,000 of Russia's 8,000,000 sq. mi., is losing some of that now. Nazis found burnt grain in the Ukraine and empty factories in industrial areas, for Russia scorched her earth as she retreated and moved war industries to safety in and behind the Urals.

Still holds after four-month siege

In Oct.-Dec., Nazis thrust to within 40 miles of Moscow, but strong Russian attacks and frigid winter now force German retreat

Scene of great battle in July

Scene of great September battle

In November, Germans took Rostov, threatening Caucasus, but were driven out shortly

In Oct.-Nov., Germans drove into Crimea, but failed to take Sevastopol or cross Kerch isthmus

British troops stood ready in Iran to aid in Caucasus defense

To Pacific: 4500 Miles

GERMAN PENETRATION
First Three Months
Second Three Months

German Thrusts
German Retreats

SCALE OF MILES
0   200

Just four weeks after the loss of *Bismarck*, Hitler launched Operation Barbarossa, his invasion of the Soviet Union. Although the Germans achieved remarkable successes in the first few months of the campaign, Hitler had sealed his doom by adding the Soviets to his list of enemies.

Soviets. This was a remarkable suggestion, since Churchill had always been a strong opponent of Soviet communism. Churchill explained his view:

> We will never parley, we will never negotiate with Hitler or any of his gang. We shall fight him by land, we shall fight him by sea, we shall fight him in the air, until,

with God's help, we have rid the earth of his shadow and
liberated its peoples from his yoke. Any man or state
who fights on against Nazism will have our aid. And
man or state who marches with Hitler is our foe. . . .
That is our policy and that is our declaration. It therefore follows that we shall give whatever help we can to
Russia and the Russian people.[28]

The United States was already sending aid to Great
Britain, through a policy known as Lend-Lease. The Lend-
Lease policy allowed the United States to help supply Great
Britain with military equipment, while still technically
remaining neutral. Great Britain now sent aid to the Soviets,
routing its convoys through the Arctic Sea to the northern
ports of Murmansk and Archangel. As the Germans continued their massive drive into the Soviet Union, and as the
Soviets kept up their desperate defense, the supplies arriving
in the north became more and more vital each day.

German U-boats naturally went after the British
convoys, but the U-boats' major thrust was still in the North
Atlantic. In addition, while the Germans continued to sink
tons upon tons of British shipping, enough British convoys
got through to preserve the vital sea links between the
United States and Great Britain, and then between Great
Britain and Russia. Had the *Bismarck* triumphed on its first
voyage, and had Admiral Lutjens indeed been able to unite
the *Bismarck*, *Gneiseneau*, and *Scharnhorst* in one great
fleet, the battle for the North Atlantic might have been
quite different.

Roosevelt had correctly predicted that the Nazis aimed
for world domination. He predicted, too, that they would
fail if Great Britain and its friends controlled the seas. That
was the single element that held Great Britain and its
supporters together during the year of June 1940 to June
1941, in which the British fought alone. The sinking of the

Bismarck was a small but important part of the turning of the tide that took place in mid-1941.

In April 1941, Hitler faced only one enemy: Great Britain. He was making progress against the British, but was impatient. By July 1941, Hitler faced two enemies: Great Britain and the Soviet Union. He was making great progress against the Soviets, but he had no idea of the vast forces that Stalin would eventually bring to bear against him. By mid-December 1941, Hitler had three enemies: Great Britain, the Soviet Union, and the United States. His Japanese ally had made a preemptive strike against the U.S. naval base at Pearl Harbor, and on December 8, the U.S. Congress had declared war on Japan. Even though Hitler's own treaty of alliance with the Japanese did not require it, he went ahead and declared war on the United States on December 11, 1941.

Hitler forged his own demise between June and December 1941. The loss of the *Bismarck* was one of the events that foreshadowed the führer's downfall. He was neither able to control his own naval leaders, nor to act on what had been his initial reaction—that he had a bad feeling about all of it.

In 2001, Englishman Rob White reported that he and his team had located the remains of the battleship *Bismarck*. This photograph shows the ruins of the admiral's bridge, where Admiral Lutjens stood in the days before the destruction of the *Bismarck*.

The Stuff
of Legend:
Attempts to Find
the *Bismarck*

A great phantom shape resting in her grave
three miles beneath the surface.

—Robert Ballard's description of
Bismarck resting on the ocean floor

The *Bismarck* continues to haunt people's minds. There is something about the image of the super-battleship that sparks the imagination and has impelled people to try to find the sunken ship. Perhaps it is because the sinking of the *Bismarck* represented the end of the great era of battleships. A prominent naval historian explained:

95

Up to mid-1941 it could have been held that the battle-ship had maintained her ancient position as "backbone of the fleet." . . . By the end of 1941 it would have been more difficult to maintain this position. The blockade of enemy surface units was increasingly maintained by aircraft, and although their attacks frequently failed to destroy heavy ships they inflicted sufficient damage to neutralize them in port.[29]

The voyage of the *Bismarck* and the hunt that culminated in its sinking are therefore an epochal part of naval history. Almost from that day forward, it became apparent that air power would eventually master surface naval units, and that command of the air was essential to maintaining command of the seas.

Despite their obsolescence, battleships continue to fasci-nate both nautical experts and the general public. As a result, the world was jubilant to learn in 1989 that the ruins of the *Bismarck* had been discovered by the same man who had found R.M.S. *Titanic* four years earlier.

Robert Ballard, an oceanographer at the Woods Hole Oceanographic Institution, had found *Titanic* in 12,500 feet (3,810 meters) of water in 1985. His name and reputation already secure, Ballard continued his deepwater dives, and in the spring of 1988, he and his crew spent three weeks searching for evidence of the sunken *Bismarck*. Ballard searched in what is known as the Porcupine Abyssal Plain, a largely flat ocean area that contains some sudden volcanic ridges. Ballard and his crew did not find much in 1988, but when they returned in May 1989, they soon found small bits of wreckage that indicated they were on the right track. The amazing discovery came on June 8, 1989, when they found "a great phantom shape resting in her grave three miles [five kilometers] beneath the surface."[30]

Ballard's crew spent days photographing the sunken ship, which was in much better condition than they had dared to hope. Part of its front had broken off during the sinking, but most of the ship was still intact. Ballard later recalled an eerie feeling he had as he came across the massive swastika painted on *Bismarck*'s deck.

Ballard left the *Bismarck* alone in 1989. The world thrilled to the news that it had been found, just over 48 years after its sinking. The *Bismarck* rested undisturbed until 2001, when another search team went after the wreck. Underwater photography had greatly improved between 1989 and 2001, and British journalists David Mearns and Rob White wanted to capture the best images possible of the sunken battleship.

Mearns and White spent several years interviewing survivors, examining key documents at the British admiralty, and working from old maps and charts. They felt confident that they could locate the remains of *Hood* in the Denmark Strait, but found that the only way their expedition could be funded was if it also searched for the remains of *Bismarck*. So, in the early summer of 2001, Mearns, White, and their associates boarded MV *Northern Horizon*, which carried the submersible *Ocean Explorer*. Armed with a large amount of scientific data, as well as anecdotal evidence provided by survivors, Mearns and White searched first for the *Bismarck*.

They had clues in the reports given by Robert Ballard and his 1989 crew. Ballard, however, had purposely kept the exact location of *Bismarck* a mystery. Mearns and White also agreed that it would be best to keep treasure and souvenir hunters away from the site; Mearns and White pledged to both the *Hood* and *Bismarck* survivors that they would not touch the sunken ships or remove any material from them.

Mearns and White found the remains of *Bismarck*

Robert Ballard of the Woods Hole Oceanographic Institution is today's foremost finder of sunken vessels. Here he points out the features of Jason Sr., an underwater robot.

early in July 2001. The first thing that was picked up on the screens aboard the ship were a pair of leather boots, "a chilling and poignant reminder that we were working around a mass grave for 2,131 men."[31] As the hours passed, Mearns and White were able to identify much more of the ghostly ship and its remains than had ever been catalogued by Robert Ballard, showing that nautical technology advances constantly. Mearns and White were able to pick out the admiral's bridge where Gunther Lutjens had stood and the shattered gun turrets that had been hit by dozens of British shells. They even found the very hatch in the aft gun director through which Baron von Mullenheim-Rechberg had been able to escape. The filming took several days, at the end of which Mearns and White were confident that they had found most of what would be needed to make interpretations about *Bismarck*.

David Mearns had previously traveled to Germany and met with members of the *Kameradschaft Schlachtschiff Bismarck*, the organization of the surviving members of *Bismarck*'s crew. The formal memorial to *Bismarck* and its crew is located on the grounds of the Bismarck family estate in Hamburg. A plaque was put together, with an inscription to the 2,246 men who were on board *Bismarck* when it sank (their names are in a compact disk that is encased within the stone tablet). Mearns and White dropped the tablet on the admiral's bridge of *Bismarck*, on the ocean floor.

First, and most important, Mearns and White confirmed that four major holes blasted by torpedoes dealt the final blow. Four gaping holes were found in the hull: two on the starboard side and two on the port. *Bismarck* might well have sunk anyway, but the shots from H.M.S. *Dorsetshire* sealed its fate. Second, whether the German crew members did anything to scuttle *Bismarck* or not, it would have gone down.

After making their conclusions, Mearns and White were off to the Denmark Strait to find the remains of *Hood*. They found *Hood* on July 20, 2001. Almost immediately, Ted Briggs was airlifted to the MV *Northern Horizon*. Briggs had waited more than 60 years for the day when he could pay his final respects to his lost shipmates. Briggs handled the lever that dropped the tablet of commemoration for those who perished in the icy waters: "In memory of our shipmates, husbands, fathers, brothers, and all relatives from the HMS *Hood* Association."

Mearns and White were able to lay to rest some, but not all, of the mystery that surrounds *Hood*'s end. It seems almost certain that *Hood* was damaged in the early part of the battle by shells fired by *Prinz Eugen*, but whether the shell that plunged through its bow came from the *Prinz Eugen* or the *Bismarck* is not known.

A great epic continues. Although *Bismarck* and *Hood* have both been found and photographed, something remains elusive about their last moments. The great chase and battle, too, continue to stir controversy and questions. Some of those questions are: Why did Hitler allow Admiral Raeder to send the ships out at all? Why did Admiral Lutjens decline to top off *Bismarck*'s fuel in Norway? Why did Lutjens refuse to allow Captain Lindemann to pursue the *Prince of Wales* after *Hood* was sunk? How could the British admiralty have steered Admiral Tovey in the wrong direction? What might have happened had Lutjens maintained radio silence, rather than fire off a long communication to Berlin on the morning of May 25?

These questions will not go away. That is because the fate of the *Bismarck* was determined by men acting on the spur of the moment. Despite all the innovations then available in radar, wireless radio, and communications, the ocean continues to befuddle even the best navigators at times.

At long last, with more than 60 years' distance, some statements may be made with certainty. The German navy was desperate to act. Hitler's intuition was good, but he failed to follow up on it. The British admiralty did its best, but came close to missing the target. If not for the heroic actions of a dozen or so Swordfish pilots, *Bismarck* might have made it to the coast of France.

Today, *Bismarck* and *Hood* lie at the bottom of the sea. That may seem fitting, since the age of great battleships is long past. Only the actions of the 4,000 men aboard the two ships remain to stir people's memories of a time when men fought and died aboard ships of iron and steel.

1918	H.M.S. *Hood* is launched; World War I ends with German defeat.
1919	The Versailles treaty states that Germany shall have no navy in the future.
1933	Adolf Hitler becomes German chancellor; Franklin Roosevelt becomes U.S. president.
1936	Work begins on the *Bismarck*.

1939

February 14	*Bismarck* is dedicated.
August 28	Hitler makes a surprising nonaggression pact with the Soviet Union; this gives him a free hand in Western Europe.
September 1	Hitler invades Poland, starting World War II.

1940

April	Hitler invades and conquers Norway.
May 10	Winston Churchill becomes British prime minister; Nazi forces invade France.
June 1	British ships evacuate troops from Dunkirk, France.
June 30	All resistance in France ceases; Great Britain stands alone.
August	German Luftwaffe begins aerial bombardment of Great Britain.
September	Hitler shifts the direction of aerial attacks to London.
October	British pilots begin to win the Battle of Britain in the skies.
December	Hitler tells his top generals that he intends to attack the Soviet Union in the spring of 1941.

1941

March	Italian dictator Benito Mussolini invades Greece, encountering heavy resistance.
April	German troops conquer Greece and Yugoslavia.
May 5	Hitler visits the *Bismarck* at Gotenhafen.
May 18	*Bismarck* leaves its mooring.
May 19	*Bismarck* and *Prinz Eugen* form a new task force.
May 20	*Bismarck* heads toward Norway; Nazi invasion of Crete begins.
May 21	*Bismarck* is spotted by British aerial reconnaissance.
May 22	*Bismarck* crosses the North Sea in bad weather.
May 23	*Bismarck* enters the Denmark Strait, heading south; Admiral John Tovey commences a massive coordination of British naval forces.

May 24	Battle of Iceland; *Bismarck* destroys H.M.S. *Hood* in a short battle; Nazi invasion of Crete builds to a climax; *Bismarck* is attacked by British Swordfish planes.
May 25	*Bismarck* and *Prinz Eugen* separate; *Bismarck* shakes off its pursuers and heads for the coast of France; British intelligence picks up *Bismarck*'s trail, but Tovey and others head in the wrong direction.
May 26	An American-made Catalina seaplane locates *Bismarck*; British pursuit is reoriented in correct direction; attack by Swordfish planes damages *Bismarck*'s rudder.
May 27	Crippled *Bismarck* is attacked by a British fleet; attack ends with *Bismarck*'s sinking at 10:40 A.M.; President Roosevelt delivers stirring radio address, declaring an unlimited state of emergency.
June 1	The last British defenders are evacuated from Crete; Germans take the island, but at a heavy price; *Prinz Eugen* arrives safely in Brest, France.
June 22	Hitler attacks the Soviet Union.
December 5	Germans bog down just short of Moscow.
December 6	Soviets begin a fierce counterattack.
December 7	Japanese bomb U.S. naval base at Pearl Harbor, Hawaii.
December 11	Hitler declares war on the United States.

CHAPTER 2: GERMANY VERSUS BRITAIN

1. *The New York Times*, February 15, 1939.
2. Quoted at http://www.ugcs.caltech.edu/ ~phoenix/ fortune/bigquotes, accessed January 2, 2003.
3. David J. Bercuson and Holger H. Herwig, *The Destruction of the Bismarck*. New York: Overlook Press, 2001, p. 14.

CHAPTER 3: BREAKOUT TO THE DENMARK STRAIT

4. Winston S. Churchill, *The Second World War, vol. 3, The Grand Alliance*. London: Cassell & Company, 1950, p. 285.
5. David J. Bercuson and Holger H. Herwig, *The Destruction of the Bismarck*. New York: Overlook Press, 2001, p. 64.
6. Ibid., p. 67.
7. Ibid., p. 80.

CHAPTER 4: THE MIGHTY H.M.S. *HOOD*

8. David Mearns and Rob White, *Hood and Bismarck: The Deep-Sea Discovery of an Epic Battle*. Channel 4 Books, 2001, p. 12.
9. David J. Bercuson and Holger H. Herwig, *The Destruction of the Bismarck*. New York: Overlook Press, 2001, p. 76.
10. David J. Bercuson and Holger H. Herwig, *The Destruction of the Bismarck*. New York: Overlook Press, 2001, p. 75.

CHAPTER 5: BATTLES OF ICELAND AND CRETE

11. Baron Burkard von Mullenheim-Rechberg, *Battleship Bismarck: A Survivor's Story*, trans. Jack Sweetman. Naval Institute Press, 1980, p. 109.
12. David Mearns and Rob White, *Hood and Bismarck: The Deep-Sea Discovery of an Epic Battle*. Channel 4 Books, 2001, p. 103.
13. C.S. Forester, *The Last Nine Days of the Bismarck*. Boston: Little, Brown and Company, 1959, p. 54.
14. Ibid., pp. 66–67.
15. Winston S. Churchill, *The Second World War, vol. 3, The Grand Alliance*. London: Cassell & Company, 1950, p. 293.

CHAPTER 6: TURN FOR FRANCE

16. David J. Bercuson and Holger H. Herwig, *The Destruction of the Bismarck*. New York: Overlook Press, 2001, p. 176.

CHAPTER 7: LOST IN THE GREAT OCEAN

17. David J. Bercuson and Holger H. Herwig, *The Destruction of the Bismarck*. New York: Overlook Press, 2001, p. 245.
18. C.S. Forester, *The Last Nine Days of the Bismarck*. Boston: Little, Brown and Company, 1959, pp. 107–108.
19. Baron Burkard von Mullenheim-Rechberg, *Battleship Bismarck: A Survivor's Story*, trans. Jack Sweetman. Naval Institute Press, 1980, p. 170.

CHAPTER 8: IN FOR THE KILL

20. Baron Burkard von Mullenheim-Rechberg, *Battleship Bismarck: A Survivor's Story*, trans. Jack Sweetman. Naval Institute Press, 1980, p. 197.
21. Winston S. Churchill, *The Second World War, vol. 3, The Grand Alliance*. London: Cassell & Company, 1950, p. 319.
22. Ibid.
23. Von Mullenheim-Rechberg, pp. 227–228.
24. Louis P. Lochner, *What About Germany?* New York: Dodd Mead & Company, 1942, p. 285.

CHAPTER 9: HITLER VERSUS ROOSEVELT

25. "Address of the President Delivered by Radio from the White House," http://www.mhric.org/ fdr/chat17.html, accessed January 3, 2003.
26. Ibid.
27. The Avalon Project at the Yale Law School, "Proclamation of Unlimited National Emergency," 1998, http://www.yale.edu/ lawweb/avalon/presiden/proclamations/ frproc01.htm, accessed January 3, 2003.
28. Reported in *New York Times* on May 29, 1941.

CHAPTER 10: THE STUFF OF LEGEND: ATTEMPTS TO FIND THE *BISMARCK*

29. Winston S. Churchill, *The Second World War, vol. 3, The Grand Alliance*. London: Cassell & Company, 1950, p. 372.
30. Robert Ballard, "The Bismarck Found," *National Geographic*, November 1989, pp. 622–637.
31. David Mearns and Rob White, *Hood and Bismarck: The Deep-Sea Discovery of an Epic Battle*. Channel 4 Books, 2001, p. 210.

Bailey, Thomas A., and Paul B. Ryan, *Hitler versus Roosevelt: The Undeclared Naval War*. New York: The Free Press, 1979.

Ballard, Robert, "The Bismarck Found," *National Geographic*, November 1989, pp. 622–637.

Bercuson, David J., and Holger H. Herwig, *The Destruction of the Bismarck*. New York: Overlook Press, 2001.

Bruce, Anthony, and William Cogar, *An Encyclopedia of Naval History*. New York: Checkmark Books, 1998.

Churchill, Winston S., *The Second World War, vol. 3, The Grand Alliance*. London: Cassell & Company, 1950.

Forester, C.S., *The Last Nine Days of the Bismarck*. Boston: Little, Brown and Company, 1959.

Grenfell, Russell, *The Bismarck Episode*. New York: Macmillan, 1949.

Halstead, Ivor, *Heroes of the Atlantic: The British Merchant Navy Carries on!* New York: E. P. Dutton & Company, 1942.

Kershaw, Ian, *Hitler: 1936–1945, Nemesis*. New York: W. W. Norton & Company, 2000.

Krist, Ernst, and Hans Speier, *German Radio Propaganda: Report on the Broadcasts During the War*. New York: Oxford University Press, 1944.

Lochner, Louis P., *What About Germany?* New York: Dodd, Mead & Company, 1942.

Mearns, David, and Rob White, *Hood and Bismarck: The Deep-Sea Discovery of an Epic Battle*. Channel 4 Books, 2001.

The New York Times, various dates throughout 1939, 1940, and 1941.

Shirer, William, *The Rise and Fall of the Third Reich*. New York: Touchstone Books, 1990.

Von de Porten, Edward P., *The German Navy in World War II*. New York: Thomas Y. Crowell Company, 1969.

Von Mullenheim-Rechberg, Baron Burkard, *Battleship Bismarck: A Survivor's Story*, trans. Jack Sweetman. Naval Institute Press, 1980.

page:

Samuel Willard Crompton teaches both American history and Western Civilization at Holyoke Community College in Massachusetts. He is the author or editor of more than 20 books, with subjects that range from lighthouses to spiritual leaders of world history. He has a special interest in nautical topics, and likes to sail off the Maine coast when he has the time.

Caspar W. Weinberger was the fifteenth secretary of defense, serving under President Ronald Reagan from 1981 to 1987. Born in California in 1917, he fought in the Pacific during World War II then went on to pursue a law career. He became an active member of the California Republican Party and was named the party's chairman in 1962. Over the next decade, Weinberger held several federal government offices, including chairman of the Federal Trade Commission and secretary of health, education, and welfare. Ronald Reagan appointed him to be secretary of defense in 1981. He became one of the most respected secretaries of defense in history and served longer than any previous secretary except for Robert McNamara (who served 1961–1968). Today, Weinberger is chairman of the influential *Forbes* magazine.